THE 24:HOUR MAN!*

FOREWORD: For Women

I am not sure what surprises me more, the incredible number of relationship books directed at women (which imply that they are to blame for relationship problems) or the minuscule number aimed at men. But let me make it clear that I don't believe there is anything wrong with women; in fact, I believe women are absolutely <u>amazing</u>! However, if some women were "broken" and these books were able to "fix" them, women would still have to deal with "broken" men! That is to say, if you were to adjust your car's alignment, you wouldn't be in any better shape if all the tires were flat! The only books women need (along with the Bible and this one) are ones that help them cope with bad relationships and books that offer comfort when their relationships end. This book will teach women and their daughters what qualities to look for in a good mate and what to teach their sons so they'll know what it means to be a man, a 24:Hour Man!* Make sure <u>EVERY</u> male you know reads this book!

FOREWORD: For Men

It is my belief that the only thing wrong with most men is that they did not have proper role models as children. Therefore, most men simply were not taught what it means to be a good husband or friend. The few men who were raised in the traditional two-parent home can still find good advice in this book. For the other 90%, <u>read quickly</u>! I don't think it's necessary to browbeat or lecture anyone, what most people need is enlightenment. That's the aim of this book, to show men how to uncover the great light they possess. Also to encourage, as is demonstrated by the first hour: <u>Every Man is Great</u>!

*Sources: The Bible, Life and Logic

THE 24:HOUR MAN!*

HOUR 1:	Every Man is Great!	page: 1
HOUR 2:	What is a 24:Hour Man?	page: 17
HOUR 3:	Diamonds and Flowers	page: 30
HOUR 4:	Oak Trees and Gold	page: 35
HOUR 5:	The Dance of Marriage	page: 37
HOUR 6:	Tightrope Walker	page: 43
HOUR 7:	Money Comma, Everything Else	page: 47
HOUR 8:	The Blame Game	page: 55
HOUR 9:	Myth Busting	page: 59
HOUR 10:	Farmer John	page: 65
HOUR 11:	Marathon Runner	page: 67
HOUR 12:	Real Love	page: 69
HOUR 13:	Check Please!	page: 74
HOUR 14:	Lexus	page: 77
HOUR 15:	20 Reasons Wives Should <u>Not</u> Work Away From Home!	page: 81
HOUR 16:	100% Logical	page: 91
HOUR 17:	Step One: Financial Stability	page: 103
HOUR 18:	Step Two: PYW, F!	page: 105
HOUR 19:	How to Pamper Your Wife	page: 106
HOUR 20:	Dr. Phil A 23:Hour Man	page: 110
HOUR 21:	4 Powerful Relationship Strengthening Techniques	page: 122
HOUR 22:	The Golden Rose	page: 126
HOUR 23:	Advice For Single Men	page: 131
HOUR 24:	The Sun!	page: 154
40 MINUTES:	Random Thoughts	page: 158
HOUR 25:	**For Women Only!**	**page: 178**

*Sources: The Bible, Life and Logic

HOUR 1:

EVERY MAN IS GREAT!

¹ **I've** always wanted to invent or discover something amazing, like gold or diamonds (or chocolate), something useful that virtually everyone could benefit from. Maybe this desire to create came from our creator. We are, after all, an image of him, one of his greatest inventions. We are so incredibly designed that even in our present imperfect state, there seems to be no limit to what we are capable of accomplishing. But strangely, as "great" as we are, one thing many of us aren't capable of doing consistently is getting along with each other, especially when it comes to marriage.

² In my long search to "discover something amazing", I stumbled upon something useful, something virtually everyone can benefit from. I found the inner light that makes every man (and woman) great! More specifically, I discovered how to use that light. Also, while digging through the rubble of my broken relationships and focusing primarily on my many mistakes, I found the secrets to improving them, by using our inner light! Combining these discoveries with logic and the wisdom from the Bible, I decided to "invent" a book, for men, to show them how to improve any relationship. To show men how quickly our relationships can improve simply by changing the way we give our light!

> **Sometimes it seems like you can't change anything.**
> **Sometimes by changing yourself, you change everything.**
> Author unknown

³ If you search the internet for books on relationships, you'll get hundreds of results. You've probably read many of them and learned that men are from Mars, Pennsylvania and women are from Venus, Texas.[1] But what else did you learn about relationships? Do you recall what you read? Did it work? Probably not, since the book you're reading, although a guide to self-improvement is also designed to improve relationships. (As you read this book circle the paragraph numbers that has information that you find especially useful.)

⁴ Although, you can find good advice in many relationship books, the problem with most of them is that they focus on "patching up" problems. The authors don't explain (or don't know) what causes the problems, or how to prevent them. They don't explain why friendships end or why love fades and dies. They all attempt to help you regain lost love. The few books that succeed in helping couples rekindle the spark fail to show them how to maintain the fire. They don't show you how to use the light we all possess.

⁵ As you have probably learned, even if you are able to regain the love, intimacy, and commitment you once had, it's not long before the fighting and arguing returns. Is commitment the problem? I don't think so; everyone knows what it means when you say the words "I do". Marriage doesn't sneak up on you like the flu; you know who gave you the (love) bug. (Bad analogy, but you get the point.) Is a lack of love the problem? Plenty of couples break up even though they feel love and passion for each other and many couples continue to have intimate moments **after** the breakup.

⁶ This means that, for at least a few moments, couples can be very loving to each other. So why can't they maintain it? Judging by the vast number of relationship books that focus on women, it would appear that women are to blame for the high number of marital problems and divorces. I, however, am not one of those who point the finger at women, in fact, I believe that:

Women are rarely the initial problem in a bad marriage, just as passengers are rarely the cause of auto accidents.

⁷ Because women are usually targeted by relationship books, it implies (intentionally or not) that they are the main cause of the problems and that they need "fixing". (It also seems that the finger is pointed at women simply because the author knows that women are more likely to purchase the book!) Virtually all women go into marriage with a pure heart and are eager to do what's necessary to make it work. They don't need fixing or blaming. The only mistake many women make is marrying men who can't and/or won't fully support them financially, spiritually, and emotionally.

⁸ Can a woman single-handedly rescue her marriage? Possibly, but that would require her to add the job of actress to her already long resume. She would have to go against her natural emotions by pretending to be happy when she or her husband is sad. To laugh when she feels like crying. She

has to convince everyone that the tears on her face are tears of joy. She must sound believable when she has to tell the bill collectors that the check is in the mail. She must heroically spend every second of every day trying to please her husband, but even then the odds are against her.

9   The role of "husband" or hero is not a character women want to play, but many women are forced to. They are fierce defenders of their families and will quickly take the lead in their marriage if they feel it is in danger. If their marriage has financial problems they won't hesitate to help by taking on second and third jobs. This heavy workload often puts a woman's health at risk and often her marriage as well, because many men don't perceive this as a loving act. They instead believe they've been insulted or dethroned. They don't understand that women will quickly do whatever they can to save their marriage, even if it means sacrificing their own identity by taking the male role in the relationship. In most cases, a woman's reaction to danger is motivated out of pure love for her family.

No need to point fingers

10   Trying to determine who is causing the problems in your relationship is not the point of this book. What you want to know is how to fix the problems and keep them from returning! If the title of this book isn't a big enough clue as to who is going to fix the problems, let me make one thing perfectly clear: this book's sole intention is to help **men** understand that the only way their relationships will improve is if they improve.[2] Not because men are the cause of all the problems, but because the man is the leader of his family. It's the husband's job to fix any problem that arises, if he can, no matter who or what caused it.

11   One thing that makes this book different from other self-help books is that you will learn EXACTLY what to do to have healthy relationships and how to maintain them. You will learn that the all-important first step for all successful marriages is EXACTLY the same; there are virtually no exceptions! (I'll explain what the first step is in a moment.) Although I make no promises that all your relationships will be successful (it takes the cooperation of everyone involved to have a good relationship), I do promise that if you follow the advice and tips in this book, people will want to be a part of your life. And you will at least see an improvement in all your relationships.

If I'm so great...

12 As stated on the cover, every man thinks he's great. But if we truly are, why do we fail at seemingly simple things, like getting along with each other and more specifically with our mates? Many men successfully run businesses with hundreds or thousands of employees, but can't manage a successful relationship with one woman! (This gives many men the FALSE idea that women are complicated and hard to deal with. See Hour: 23, pg. 144 para.479-482)

13 This can lead to great confusion. We say to ourselves, "Why can't I maintain a simple, happy relationship? I'm not perfect, but my heart is in the right place most of the time. I never feel in control, my relationships rarely feel stable. What can I do to help my marriage?" When we're confused, it becomes very easy for us to begin to doubt ourselves and our abilities.

14 Let me state again that men (and women) are one of God's greatest creations. Every man is great, because every man is the image of God! Men are designed to accomplish virtually anything. Keep that in mind whenever you doubt your abilities. Never say to yourself, "I can't do this". Instead, simply say, "I need to focus on getting this done" and then search for the solution to accomplish it. Rarely is it a matter of "IF" you can accomplish something, it's almost always "WHEN" will you accomplish it!

15 In fact, we are so masterfully designed that it is virtually impossible for us **not** to succeed in improving our personal abilities, as long as we get the proper education and never give up! Whether it's learning a new language, learning to play the piano or losing weight, if you have the necessary guidance and never give up, it is impossible not to succeed! It's just a matter of when will you succeed![3]

16 Maintaining happy, long-lasting relationships also require that we get the proper education and never give up! Unfortunately, friendship and marriage are not taught in school. Often, we learn how to be a good friend through trial and error. We almost expect to lose a few friends along the way, but we continue to grow like an evergreen that loses a few leaves.

> **Friends are like pendants that hang freely on a necklace.
> Marriage is a gold ring with one diamond
> permanently bonded to it.**
> T24HM!*2014

17 Marriage, on the other hand, is a unique relationship, entered into with permanence in mind. Adjustments have to be made, but living happily ever after is usually the aim. Many couples start marriage with this simple goal, relying on blind faith that they can survive the ups and downs. Unfortunately, many couples don't make it through the months or years of struggle and many that do survive aren't happy with what their marriage has become. Nobody wants to be in a bad relationship, but few seem to know the secrets for a successful one. (You'll learn the secrets to maintaining good relationships and the importance of helping others by the time you finish this book.)

18 It is very important that you know how relationships and marriage in particular, operate **before** you start one! Men must understand that marriage comes with many responsibilities, but first and foremost, a man must provide **full financial support** for his household. Knowing that he must provide for his family and being financially able to do so, are the first things a man must know before even considering marriage. Once a man decides he's ready for marriage he must understand that:

It is virtually impossible to be a good husband without money!

19 I define a good husband as a financially stable man who understands that it is his job to take care of all the needs of his family. His job includes making sure his family is emotionally and physically secure. He also knows that he must make it clear to his wife that he will fully support her lovingly, willingly, and consistently, forever!

20 This vow is a lot easier to keep when your finances are in order. In fact, a successful marriage **must** have financial stability. And more specifically, the **husband** must be financially stable; it is the **first** and **most important** step in establishing a successful marriage. If you are presently married and not financially stable, becoming financially stable must be one of your top priorities, because a marriage with money problems will always feel unstable! (Although financial stability is the first step for a healthy marriage, it is not the cure for every problem; financial stability is the first step in establishing and maintaining a successful marriage, not the only step.)

²¹   A good, financially stable husband needs to be giving and affectionate. He also has the very important job of protecting his family. But a man who is not financially stable is like a shade tree with no leaves; he provides limited protection. The job of "husband" or provider is virtually impossible to successfully accomplish without money and a good husband never hands the job of financially supporting the family over to his wife. Wives already have many very important jobs to do without the added responsibility of worrying about finances.

²²   All relationships have many adjustments to make before they begin to settle. However, marriage in particular, needs time, patience, and the protection of money, especially at the beginning, before it can become solid; just as freshly laid cement needs time and protection before it can harden. A new marriage, like wet cement that is not protected, will never become solid as long as it's exposed to the storm of financial insecurity.

²³   Simply knowing that you must provide for your family is not enough. You may have read everything from Dr. Phil to Dr. Seuss. And you may also have a heart of pure gold, but unless you can chip off a piece of your heart and exchange it for cold cash, your knowledge and good intentions will not be enough to properly take care of your family. Knowledge only tells you that you **should** take care of your wife and family, money allows you to do it.

²⁴   To clarify, you don't need money to be a good 24:Hour Man, but you do need money to be a good, "24 Hour" husband and father. Without money, neither you nor your wife will feel secure, therefore your marriage will not feel secure. And two insecure, financially unstable people won't stay together long (at least not happily), no matter how much they love each other.

²⁵   Of course, if you intend on being a farmer and living completely off your land, you can probably get by without money. But if you also intend on getting married, let me suggest that you fill your barn with lots of crops and brush up on your bartering skills before you take on a wife. Even then, you may still need money for things you can't grow or trade for or make yourself, like a tractor or glasses (I'll assume your wife doesn't care for Prada or Louis Vuitton). And if you or a member of your family needs medical attention, most doctors won't accept your prize hog as payment for his services. For

the other 99.9% percent of men who don't intend on being a farmer, you're going to need a steady positive cash flow if you're considering marriage.

Good men, good husbands

²⁶ Contrary to popular belief, there are plenty of good men in our society, but being a good man does not mean you are or will be a good husband. Among other things, a good man is simply a person who helps others when he can (and tries not to cause harm to anyone); no special training or super-human abilities are needed, just a willingness to be of assistance.

²⁷ A good husband also helps others when he can, but his first priority is to take care of his family. He works hard to ensure that his wife is both financially and emotionally secure. A good husband is a provider and he understands that he is solely responsible for the financial stability of his household.

²⁸ I cannot stress enough (although I'll try many times throughout this book) the importance not only of being financially stable, but being stable financially **before** marriage. For example, would you allow someone to operate on you before he had completed his training? Most people won't even allow someone to cut their hair until they are certified! So why go into marriage financially "uncertified".

²⁹ Although financial stability is the all-important first step in establishing a successful marriage, it's the loving interactions that make two unique individuals want to bond forever. When your wife wants affection, when she wants a kiss, rubbing a ten-dollar bill on her lips won't satisfy her. What she craves is the touch of a confident man. Nothing is more attractive to a woman than a confident, strong man and nothing can quench her desire for affection like his touch. When a man has enough money to provide for his family he feels strong and sure of himself.

³⁰ When a man is financially stable, he can easily play his role as provider and protector, thereby allowing his wife to be the loving helper she was designed to be. Of course, many couples are financially stable and at one time were madly in love, so what causes so many relationships to fall apart?

Formula for a successful marriage[4]

31   To maintain a healthy marriage, you must give of yourself freely and consistently. Financial stability and consistent expressions of love will virtually guarantee a successful marriage. Recall the question stated earlier, "Why can't I maintain a simple, happy relationship?" Part of the reason many marriages fail is answered in the next sentence, "my heart is in the right place most of the time." Your heart can't be in the right place "most of the time"; it has to be in the right place **all** the time. Proverbs 17:17 states that "a friend is loving at all times." Wives desire and deserve to be loved at all times as well; you are her best and closest friend!

32   A strong marriage depends on a financially stable, loving husband. In fact, I believe it's the only way to have a successful marriage! And let me add one more bold statement: A woman who loves her husband will never leave him as long as he loves and fully supports her! As "proof" of that last statement, if your wife is with you now and you're **not** a loving, financially stable husband, isn't that proof of her loyalty? Do you think your wife would leave you if you fully supported her and took care of her emotional needs?

33   Even if you feel as though your marriage has reached its end and that your wife wants to leave you, the fact of the matter is, she hasn't. She's stayed with you, even though you've given her every reason to leave. What she wants from you is a reason to stay. If you give your marriage the love and financial stability it needs, your wife will stay with you as surely and as loyally as the earth stays in the gravity of the sun!

34   To guarantee a successful marriage you must **consistently** show your wife you love her, above all others and all things, (while also providing financial security). Fortunately (or unfortunately) for men, the vast majority of women don't marry for money. (I say unfortunately, because if women did require men to be financially stable before they would enter into a relationship with them, most men would strive for that goal before getting married.) Though women should be provided for and protected, what women crave is love and affection. Women will gladly struggle financially with the man they love as long as they are being loved and at least have the basic necessities.

> A woman who feels loved, feels secure.
> A woman who feels secure, feels loved.
> T24HM!*2014

35   However, don't let the fact that women love their husbands more than money be an excuse not to **fully** support them financially! Although women will show how much they love their husbands by struggling financially for years, that does not mean they should be asked or forced to do so. Would it be loving to ask a woman to marry you, knowing that you are going to struggle financially, possibly for years? I say the answer is, no! And asking her to help financially is also not a good way to start a marriage.

36   Asking your wife to work outside the home is comparable to borrowing her diamond wedding ring and using it to cut several panes of glass! Although most women are willing to assist their husbands by working outside the home and a diamond ring can easily cut glass, that's not what they were designed to do! And if you continue to use the ring for this purpose you **will** damage it![5]

37   How about a more "personal" illustration? Imagine driving to the cleaners to have your $1,000 Armani suit cleaned. As you exit your car you notice that there is dirt on the hood. Would the thought of using your suit to wipe the dirt off your car ever occur to you? Of course not, even though the suit could easily do the job. However, as stated earlier, if you regularly use something in a way it was not designed to be used, eventually you will damage it!

38   Likewise, you should never use your "Armani" wife to build a financial foundation that should have been built before you got married! If you choose to use your wife for a purpose she was not designed, you are placing her and therefore your marriage, in a very dangerous position. (To be clear, you should not **start** a marriage with the idea that your wife is going to help financially. But obviously circumstances can change during the marriage and she may have to assist in earning money. But do not let new circumstances be an excuse to reduce the love, affection, and protection she has become accustomed to! Also, keep in mind that you must assist her in maintaining the housework (or hire someone, if possible) since that job still needs to be taken care of. If her workload is increased, then yours should also. And you must **continually** show your appreciation for her assistance.)

Struggling financially leads to other problems

⁣³⁹   To make matters worse, husbands who are not financially stable often begin to suffer emotionally and physically, because of pressure and stress. A man's inability to provide for his family will obviously affect his marriage negatively. Although he may appear to be calm, he is a pitiful, lonely figure standing in the eye of a storm that was largely stirred up by his own doing or "lack of doing". Because he didn't put in the hard work necessary to build a solid financial foundation (before marriage), his household will be yet another source of turmoil and anxiety. His home-life will continue to be stressful and love-challenged until he gets his finances under control.

> **Most marriages fail <u>not</u> because of a lack of love, they fail because of a lack of money, which <u>leads</u> to a lack of love.**
> T24HM!*2014

⁣⁴⁰   A husband who is constantly stressed brings constant stress to his family. There is no such thing as a happy, financially broke husband! On the other hand, the financially stable man has the time and means to offer his wife the things she needs: protection,[6] consistent love, and affection. If you don't understand the connection between financial stability (along with consistent expressions of love) and a successful marriage, you will by the time you finish this book.

⁣⁴¹   Being a good husband doesn't mean you have to be perfect. Just as a great athlete isn't great every game and rarely, if ever, has a perfect performance. However, there is something he gives virtually every game, consistent, positive effort! That's all any wife needs from her (financially and emotionally stable) husband: consistent, positive effort, which she will interpret as true love.

⁣⁴²   Notice that I have not mentioned the role of a wife. That is because wives are a reflection of their husbands.[7] In other words, wives normally follow their husbands' lead. You are, biblically speaking, one flesh and you both drink from the same cup of life. What affects you, affects her. If you're stressed and unhappy, she'll be stressed and unhappy, but if you take the lead by loving and protecting her, she will love and protect you. That is one of the few guarantees we have in life.

⁴³ That's why it's very important to be stable financially and emotionally, **before** marriage. The marriage will follow the pattern you set. You must understand that although the responsibility of leading a family may at times be difficult, how difficult must it be for a woman to be married to a man who is unable, or unwilling to properly care for his family? Leading a family may be challenging, but after you complete this book you will understand that you are more than able to maintain a healthy, loving, and financially stable relationship.

⁴⁴ Once again, it takes more than money to be a great husband, but you can't be great without it. Becoming financially stable should be a goal of every man, whether he intends to get married or not. It may appear that I am placing all the responsibility for a successful marriage on men, but in reality, what I'm saying is that a successful marriage **begins** with a financially stable man. And a marital relationship will only remain stable as long as the husband is stable, both emotionally and financially.

What do you have to lose?

⁴⁵ Before I even finished this book I was told that my views were unrealistic and too simplistic (in other words, old-fashioned) and that I use too many generalizations.[8] Many said that people would not accept my one-size-fits-all advice, specifically, that men should be financially stable before getting married. But is it realistic to believe that you will have a long, happy marriage if you're always in the midst of financial problems, along with life's normal challenges?

⁴⁶ I agree that most men will not wait until they are financially stable to get married, but that doesn't mean I shouldn't encourage it. Just as I would encourage men to refrain from sex until marriage and concentrate on building a strong spiritual foundation, especially since it is the best way to start and maintain a happy marriage. The wise man saves and waits patiently for the things he wants, shouldn't that same plan of action apply to marriage?

⁴⁷ I also agree that being financially stable before marriage is not a 100% guarantee that you will have a happy, lasting relationship (although it raises the odds considerably, especially if you give generously). But a lack of financial stability will virtually guarantee a sad, tragic, short marriage.

⁴⁸ I was also told that relationships are not as simple as I make them out to be.⁹ I don't know if relationships are supposed to be easy, but I do believe they are easier to maintain IF you have the proper tools: financial stability, patience, understanding, etc. I also believe that marriage (or any type of relationship) is much easier to manage if you have the proper tools BEFORE you need them! For example, it's a lot easier to change a flat tire if you have the proper tools. And the job will be done a lot quicker if you have the proper tools BEFORE you need them!

⁴⁹ As to the question of whether relationships are supposed to be easy. We all have special friends with whom we immediately connected. It seems so easy and simple to have a good relationship with them. And for whatever reason, they love us seemingly unconditionally. One quality that is common among those special friends is that they all put forth the same consistent effort to maintain our friendship. What I am asking you to do is to give that same type of effort to everyone you come in contact with and especially to your wife. Be as easy to love as our special friends.

⁵⁰ Can I guarantee that your efforts will lead to instant happiness? No, but I can virtually guarantee that all your relationships will begin to improve if you become a person who gives consistently. When we make changes we can never be sure if we will receive positive results, but we can stay motivated to make those changes if we understand that:

> **Action may not always bring happiness,
> but there is no happiness without action.**
> Benjamin Disraeli

⁵¹ By trying the suggestions in this book, what do you have to lose? Will your wife love you less if you take care of her financially and emotionally? Would providing a safe and loving home make her want to spend more time in bars? Would consistently treating your wife with kindness drive her away from you? Of course not, because you would be treating her the way every woman wants to be treated; with consistent love and affection. Often, when men speak of their marriage, they proclaim that they would give their lives for their wives. I'm not asking you to give your life, just read and follow the advice in this book!

⁵² Keep in mind that although many types of relationships are discussed throughout this book (with a primary focus on marriage), the goal is improving how men give. By improving, I simply mean giving of yourself more consistently. I will stress this often. Giving makes you feel good and a byproduct of consistent giving is an improvement in all your relationships!

⁵³ As the saying goes, "when the student is ready, the teacher will appear". By reading this book, I think you are ready. But instead of thinking of me as a teacher, think of me as a friend, a brother who has made the same mistakes you've made. A brother who is striving, just as you are, to be a man in every sense of the word.

⁵⁴ Every man thinks he's great, because every man knows there is something in us that makes us feel as though we can do anything. It's no secret there is a powerful light within all of us, but it seems we've come to believe we have a limited supply of this light. Therefore, we don't freely give of ourselves. The truth of the matter is that we have unlimited power as long as we remain connected to the original power source. And we will also receive an additional jolt of energy from others and especially from our loved ones if we make sure they are "fully charged" with our love!

⁵⁵ Love, like light, must be given consistently. A little love, like a little light, is hard to see and feel. We must avoid being like a light bulb that flickers annoyingly, especially since we have a thousand watts of power in our hearts. There is no good reason to withhold the light that allows us to see and help others and allows others to see and help us.

> **Some say we only use about 10% of our mental capacity, whether or not that's true, we can always give 100% of our love.**
> T24HM!*2014

⁵⁶ We must allow the light within us to shine consistently, because giving **consistently** is the secret to improving any relationship! If every man mastered the art of consistent giving, it would go without saying that "Every Man is Great", because, like the sun, everyone would see your light, 24 hour a day. You would be the very definition of the 24:Hour Man!:

¹(para.3) ***Men are from Mars, Women are from Venus*** *(published in 1992) is a book offering many suggestions for improving husband-wife relationships.*

(Mars, Pennsylvania and Venus, Texas are actual towns in the US.)

²(para.10) *This book was written specifically to teach men the importance of giving of themselves consistently. I am under no obligation to be "PC" (politically correct), but I am obligated to be "BC" (biblically correct). As such, many men are in for a rude, but necessary awakening in the following pages. But I urge you to fight through it and accept the challenge of making up for past wrongs and rebuilding damaged relationships. Although this book was written to teach and encourage, I must at times expose past sins, not to belittle, but to show what behavior is not befitting a man of good character.*

³(para.15) *It does not matter how slowly you go so long as you do not stop.*
 - Confucius

⁴(above para.31) *A simple phrase to remember to have a good marriage:* **A woman must feel both safe and loved.** *The only way to insure those two things consistently is to be financially stable.*

Illustration: Imagine you've just bought the car of your dreams. It has every feature imaginable, but there's one problem, it has defective brakes! Would you for one second feel safe driving it? Would the smooth ride or leather interior make you feel secure? Could you fully enjoy **anything** *about your new car while driving it? The answer is obviously, no, because you know you must pay complete attention to how you drive, so as not to lose control.*

Similarly, a woman who is married to a financially unstable man does not feel safe (and therefore, does not feel fully loved). She can't give her full attention to her husband, because she has to worry about finances and the problems that are caused when money is scarce. That doesn't mean women won't try to make their marriage work, it means that they will always have their love and multitasking skills pushed to the limit.

[5] *(para.36) In Hour: 3, I compare women to diamonds and in Hour: 4, I compare men to gold. I find it interesting that if a diamond ring were indeed used to cut glass, it is the gold ring that would buckle under the pressure before the diamond. Men, and in particular husbands, are not at their best when they struggle financially, as this illustration, and life has shown. Most working-wives, though they may no longer have their original luster, will continue to work hard (continue to cut glass), as long as their husbands (the gold ring) lovingly holds onto them. In other words, as long as a man fights to keep his marriage together so will his wife.*

[6] *(para.40) I will stress often the importance of protecting and providing for your wife and helping women in general. Not because I believe they are weak and defenseless, but because they deserve an environment of safety in order to fully perform their roles as wife and mother.*

To illustrate (I will assume you are a healthy, hard-working man), imagine that you have to go to work every day in a building that had no roof and no window panes! Obviously, on clear, sunny days, you could get your work done. But what would your attitude be on days when the temperature dipped below freezing or soared above 100 degrees? How about rainy or snowy days when you have to cover your work area with a tarp? As you can imagine, your productivity would suffer, to say the least, not to mention your morale. What would you think of a company that didn't provide basic necessities? Would you look forward to working for a company that obviously didn't seem to care about your well-being?

I hope that you can see that the parallel I'm attempting to make is that the act of protecting and providing for your wife is not just a basic necessity, but a basic act of love. **There is no way your wife will feel you love and value her if you don't keep her safe,** *if you don't provide her with basic needs, like a roof over her head and affection.*

To further the point, if your wife has a job, on days when she doesn't have to go to work, she can spend time with her family and enjoy her roles as a wife and mother. But what do you think her attitude will be on days when she has to get out of a warm bed and go to work in freezing weather? Driving alone on dangerous slick roads in the early morning to a job she probably hates. Do you think she looks forward to the years ahead as the wife of a man who doesn't seem to care about her well-being? I'm sure you know the answer to those questions, which is why I will stress often that a man has to keep his wife safe and the only way he can do that consistently is if his finances are in order.

[7] (para.42) It is very important that you understand how women interact with their husbands and their environment. Wives are a reflection of their husbands love! Women naturally blend their lives with their mates and they accept the fact that they are vulnerable to the actions of the "driver" of their relationships. If you imagine that a woman is a passenger in a car, it should be easy to see that if the car is driven safely, she would feel safe and secure. And it should be easy to see that a passenger of a car that is driven recklessly would behave in an unpredictable manner. It is exactly the same with relationships; women will reflect the treatment they receive. Your relationships will go a lot smoother if you understand that women love and take care of men who love and take care of them.

[8] (para.45) While it is true that I use many generalizations throughout this book, it is done so purposefully. I realize that every woman isn't dainty, soft, and sweet; although that is my wish and also my belief that virtually every woman (if allowed) has the potential to be soft and sweet. And every man isn't big, strong, and honorable, but nature itself is a stereotype; all roses are dainty, soft, and sweet, the mighty oak is big, strong, and "honorable". It seems to me that problems occur when we step outside of generalizations; in other words, when we act inconsistently. When I bite into an apple, I want and expect it to be sweet and not to taste like an orange. When a butterfly rests on my finger I don't expect it to sting me and when I kiss a woman's lips, I want and expect them to be soft! (Call me old-fashioned)

[9] (para.48) I don't know how simple or easy relationships are supposed to be, but one of the points of this book is that everything is easier when you have the tools to complete the job. One of the "tools" you need to have a successful marital relationship is money. It is by far the most important tool you'll need to make sure your relationship stays secure. Money buys the important things like food, shelter, and clothing, as well as the small things. Even if you live a very simple life and calmly sail downstream, if you don't have an oar to help guide your way, you won't feel in control. With money you can buy the oar (the small things) that you and your family will need to steer away from danger.

HOUR 2:
WHAT IS A 24:HOUR MAN?

57 A 24:Hour Man does not say to his wife, "I heard a noise downstairs, it's your turn to see what it is" or "We have a flat tire, it's your turn to change it." What would you think of a man if you saw him sitting in a car while his wife changed a flat tire? Unfortunately, similar examples are what many men (and women) have seen all their lives; men treating women as if they were men.

58 Would the sun say to the earth, "It's your turn to illuminate the universe"? Of course not, because that's not what the earth was designed to do, but that is what the sun was designed to do. The sun does its job consistently, 24 hours a day. In like manner, a man should imitate the sun and do his "job" of being a man, consistently, 24 hours a day. Therefore, the answer to the question, "What is a 24:Hour Man?", simply stated is:

A 24:Hour Man is a Man, 24 Hours a Day!

59 What does it mean to be a man? Definitions abound. How about the masculine reflection of God? And since God is love, men must be a reflection of his love. God gives consistently, 24 hours a day. Accordingly, a 24:Hour Man is a man who gives consistently, 24 hours a day!

60 In addition to being a giving person, there is a long and varied list of manly qualities. Men of high quality are described as being intelligent, trustworthy, honest, and confident. But what makes a man, a "24:Hour Man", is not simply a list of adjectives. He demonstrates his greatness by **consistently** imitating his creator, by **consistently** giving of himself. Consistency is the key to his greatness!

⁶¹   Nothing is of any real, lasting value if it is not consistent. The 24:Hour Man is not kind sometimes or generous sometimes, he is the same, 24 hours a day. Think of all the people who have made a lasting impression on you. What is the one thing that is common among all of them? People we admire the most are all consistent givers. The 24:Hour Man is a consistent giver and like the sun, he is a source of positive light, 24 hours a day!

⁶²   Although consistent giving is very important, just as important is knowing what to give. Though it seems obvious that it is best to give a person what they want or need, instead, many people have a tendency to give what **they** want to give. It may be kind to give someone tickets to the ballet, but if he or she doesn't like to watch women dancing on their toes and men in super-tight spandex, you've wasted your money. (The "gift" could even be seen as insensitive if the receiver is unemployed and needs money.) The giver is then left confused as to why the gift wasn't well received. They failed to see that the gift wasn't something wanted or needed.

⁶³   To better understand what it means to give a person what they want, I'd like to tell you about an experience a man had with his young son. One particular day he got home early and decided to walk down the street and pick up his son early from the daycare center. He hadn't spent much time with him recently and wanted to spend some quality time with him. Soon upon arriving home his son said he wanted to go back to the daycare center.

⁶⁴   Although he was disappointed, he understood that his son enjoyed being there with his friends and he completely understood the importance of giving a person what they want, even if it hurts. With a heavy-heart, he proceeded to walk his son back to the daycare center. When he picked up his son later that day, his son happily rushed into his arms. Maybe this was his son's way of showing his appreciation for having such a caring, understanding father. The incident made him appreciate the time he spent with his son even more.

Men are like the Sun

⁶⁵ I once spoke to a group of men about relationships and one of them said that the way I spoke sounded like I wanted to be "in control" of my relationships. I was surprised that this statement came from a man who (judging by his earlier statements) was himself controlling![1] I realized from his comment and from the look on the faces of some of the other men in the audience, that most men don't know what it means to be a man and certainly not a 24:Hour Man.

⁶⁶ I asked him how many steering wheels he had in his car. Some of the men laughed, because they understood what I meant, but the man who questioned me did not. I told him that just as a car has only one steering wheel, someone has to be the driver of the relationship; someone has to be "in control".[2] When you drive a car, what you control is the car not the other passengers. If they don't like the way you drive (lead the relationship), they're free to leave (and will probably do so).

⁶⁷ His question actually implied that I believed men are supposed to be in control of women. Not only did he fail to grasp the steering wheel analogy, his question made it clear that he did not understand the role of the husband in marriage. I proceeded to tell him that I wasn't the one who decided who would be "in control" (in other words, the driver or leader) of my relationships. I told him that on the day I was born and the doctor said I was a boy, I was destined to be the leader of my family, if I had one. And just as the sun is designed to provide warmth and light for the earth, I was designed to provide kind, loving leadership, and financial support for my family.

⁶⁸ If I chose to have a family, I have **no choice** but to be the one who is "in control", not of my wife, but of the relationship. Leading the family is one of the many roles God gave men. If I (not my wife) don't lead properly, the union will fail. (There can only be one driver of a relationship, it will swerve dangerously if the couple continuously fights for control of the "steering wheel".)

⁶⁹ Just as the sun was designed for a specific purpose, the 24:Hour Man knows he is specifically designed to be a provider of light (that others will perceive as protective, comforting love). He is expected to be approachable

and kind, a source of encouragement and security. A good husband is a protector of his family, a giver of whatever is needed, 24 hours a day! And like the sun, he uses his power and energy for the benefit of everyone he comes in contact with, regardless of what he receives in return.

70   The 24:Hour Man, like the sun, never asks for anything in return for giving and yet never stops giving. The sun doesn't need anything from the earth to exist. **It is complete as it is!** The earth doesn't need the sun to exist, although it does become more beautiful as it revolves in its gravity.[3]

71   Unlike the earth, women aren't locked in into any one man's "gravity". Her husband doesn't control her; he protects and provides for her. A woman is drawn to her husband and remains near him because she wants to, not because she's forced to. The only thing a man controls is himself.

> **In life, we have control over two things,
> what we think, and what we say.**
> Author Unknown

72   The 24:Hour Man is concerned with giving whatever is necessary, not taking whatever he can take. He gives and expects nothing in return, nothing! Not respect, not love, not praise, not even thanks. Anything given to him is a bonus. He knows that when he gives of himself, he is doing nothing extraordinary. That's what he is supposed to do, what he was specifically designed to do. He is more concerned with helping others than receiving praise. **He is complete as he is!**

73   It is very important that you understand and accept what was stated in the last paragraph. A 24:Hour Man gives freely and "expects nothing in return"![4] The sun gives, "knowing" it will not receive anything in return and yet, it never stops giving. It doesn't give because it wants to receive something. It gives simply because that's what it was designed to do. (Unlike the sun, you **will** receive all the love, praise, and respect you deserve. Just don't look for it. I can promise you from experience that while it may not come when you think it should or in the form you expect, you will be rewarded for your efforts. Thanks may only be shown with a smile, but since you are complete as you are, isn't that more than enough?)

You are the Sun!

74   If you expect thanks, or repayment for the things you do for others and don't receive it, it's easy to become resentful and withhold your "light". But don't forget that you are the sun, the brightest star in your family's universe. Don't let anything stop you from giving your warmth. The sun radiates just as much in the winter as it does in the summer. It shines just as bright at night as it does during the day! It never stops giving. It never stops shining. It never stops being what it is, so don't stop being who you are. Don't withhold your light for any reason. The 24:Hour Man is a consistent giver of positive light!

75   What if you woke up one morning and discovered that the sun was gone? That it left because it "felt" taken for granted, that it wasn't receiving the thanks it deserved. Soon after you realized what had happened, you would begin making plans to go on without it.

76   When a man leaves his wife for any reason,[5] he causes incredible damaged to the relationship. He has made the relationship even more unstable by showing that he is willing to leave at any time, for any reason. He shows her that he is temperamental, fragile, immature, and needy, and that he expects to be "paid back" for everything he does.

77   Worst of all, it tells his wife that he doesn't love her and that he is willing to abandon her if she doesn't give him what he thinks he deserves. Even if she accepts him back, she has to mentally prepare herself for the next time he thinks he's not being appreciated. Some women don't wait for the next time and instead leave before he gets another chance. Others stay in the relationship, but have a difficult time reconnecting emotionally.

78   The reverse is also damaging. If the sun "stood still", shining its light on the same side of the earth, "waiting for praise", the results would be devastating. The sun would soon be viewed as a necessary evil. Likewise, a husband that hovers over his wife until she shows appreciation for the light he "graciously" bestows upon her, will eventually devastate his marriage.

⁷⁹ The intense light (or heat) he gives will soon become too hot to bear, she will begin to find the night (time away from her husband) more desirable. But it won't be long before the icy twilight hours of loneliness force her to seek the warmth and comfort she craves and deserves. In the darkness of night, any light appears comforting. She may find herself in the arms of any man who offers even a flicker of solace. Her ever-shining husband will then tell every ear that will listen that his ungrateful wife abandoned him, although he gave her everything she needed and that all he wanted from her was a little appreciation.

⁸⁰ When you expect something in return for giving, people are less likely to thank you and are less likely to accept anything from you in the future. Your gifts seem less desirable; no one wants gifts with strings attached. This is why I stress that you must give freely, like the sun. The 24:Hour Man gives freely and consistently, and expects **nothing** in return! He doesn't need anything because, **he is complete as he is!**

⁸¹ The 24:Hour Man is too busy rendering assistance to linger, waiting for praise and pats on the back. Like the sun, he disappears beyond the horizon, shedding light on anyone in need of comfort. He is always as welcome as a new day.

> **Spread love everywhere you go.**
> **Let no one come to you without leaving happier.**
> Mother Teresa

⁸² When giving takes over your personality, giving itself will be one of your rewards.⁶ You may also receive an unnecessary bonus in the form of smiles and tears of joy. But if you truly are complete as you are, what can anyone give you that you don't already have? The feeling of being a provider and protector is very powerful and gratifying. It's not a feeling anyone can give you. It's a feeling you get when you give, which means that when you give, you are actually rewarding yourself!

⁸³ There are of course, many men who lovingly support their families, but many men do not. Numerous marriages have women placed in a position they have no choice but to assume; being responsible financially for their household. This usually occurs because many men don't wait until they are stable financially before they decide to get married.

84   Instead, many men get married without a solid financial foundation and expect their wives to help them with the finances. When women take on this burden, they often sacrifice their health and something just as important, their femininity and beauty; the very thing that attracted their husbands in the first place. And in an ironic twist, when a woman begins to excel as the leader of the family, she is called bossy and a control freak, among many other names.

85   On the other hand, if she is not successful at running the household she is also criticized! It's a classic no-win situation that is the direct result of a man getting married before he was financially stable. He has created a "control freak" because **he** lacks control. She wears the pants only because he refuses to. Make no mistake about it, a bossy wife does not exist without a financially weak husband who has resigned from his job. She didn't take his position, he quit![7]

86   Many men believe that they need their wives to work, because they think it will make the family more financially secure. It may in some cases, but at what cost? I strongly believe that if a married woman works outside the home (a typical 9 to 5 or even worse, the "graveyard shift"), in time, it will not only make the marriage weaker, it will also weaken her husband!

87   For example, imagine a man lying on a bench lifting weights. He can lift 200 pounds. His wife, standing at the front of the bench, begins to assist him by lifting the weights also. They split the (financial) work in half, each lifting about 100 pounds. Together they can lift the weight (pay the bills) with ease and they gradually add more weight. Together they can now lift 300 pounds!

88   But what if his wife can no longer assist him, for any number of reasons: injury, termination, illness or pregnancy? Because of her "help" his (financial) muscles have now become accustomed to only lifting 150 pounds (half of the 300 pounds). He has come to depend on her assistance. He has **actually** become weaker. And to make matters worse, he now has the added responsibility of lifting more weight (300 pounds instead of 200) than he was previously lifting! What was once "assistance" from his wife has now become a necessity.

⁸⁹ It's easy to see that if a working wife has to stop working, the marriage will quickly head downhill. The pressure of mounting bills (and life's normal challenges) will put tremendous strain on the marriage, but this is only the tip of the proverbial iceberg. There are many more dangers that marriages face when wives work outside the home, as you'll see in Hour: 15.

⁹⁰ The 24:Hour Man does not need help to support his family. He has taken steps before marriage to insure that he can easily provide for his household and he is prepared for emergencies. He never expects his wife to concern herself with finances, because he knows that is not the role of a wife. He knows that more harm than good comes from asking his wife to work outside the home. As stated earlier, many men treat women as if they were men, expecting them to be as strong and tough as they are and yet remain soft and beautiful! It doesn't take a genius to figure out that:

It is impossible for a woman to work as long and hard as a man, and retain all her feminine qualities.

⁹¹ In case you hadn't noticed, women aren't men. Not to say that women are fragile and weak. I learned at a young age just how physically strong females can be. I remember an incident when I was about 24 years old. I was arm wrestling a few teenagers and I boasted that no one could last more than 3 seconds before I pinned them. After taking on all challengers I rested my mighty Herculean arm. I was approached a short time later by a small, thin teenage girl whom I had never met. She shyly asked if she could arm wrestle me. I coolly said yes and prepared to take on my petite foe. To say that I was over-confident would be an understatement, though not unjustified, as I outweighed my tiny opponent by 50 pounds!

⁹² I don't think I would have brought this story up had she beaten me, because the thought of almost losing still haunts me to this day! The match lasted about 6 seconds. At the 3 second mark I hadn't moved her an inch, but she eventually gave in. Although I wasn't in danger of losing (at least that's what I tell myself), my "victory", the epitome of winning ugly, taught me some valuable lessons: One, women (and young girls) are not weak and two, women can do virtually anything a man can do, just not as long in some cases.

⁹³ Wives are more than capable assistants for their husbands; they show their value in a variety of ways. For the 24:Hour Man, a wife is like a million dollars in a savings account, always accruing interest and always available for emergencies. And just as you're not supposed to "live off" your savings, a 24:Hour Man does not live off his wife. He has a solid financial foundation and only uses his savings (or his wife) in extreme situations.[8]

⁹⁴ Although every man should strive to be financially stable, let me stress that this goal only becomes paramount as it pertains to marriage and children. In other words, you don't need money to be a 24:Hour Man, but you do need money to be a good 24:Hour Husband and Father! The 24:Hour Man has many good qualities that he exhibits consistently, here are some of them:

Qualities of the 24:Hour Man!

Religious

⁹⁵ A religious man knows that he is required to give the love he receives from God freely, generously, and consistently. He reads the Bible regularly and is therefore constantly reminded of his responsibilities to God and others. True religion strengthens and counteracts the negativity we encounter every day.

Kind

⁹⁶ One of the most outstanding qualities of the 24:Hour Man is kindness; it's what makes him approachable. I believe most people are kind, but most people wait for someone to show them kindness before they respond. Not the 24:Hour Man, he takes the initiative and practices "proactive kindness". He doesn't wait for someone to show him kindness, he makes the first move. He is always looking for ways to brighten someone's day.

Generous

⁹⁷ The 24:Hour Man is always willing to lend a hand. Whether it is financial assistance or advice or a kind word, his giving nature always lifts

your spirits. It's said that a generous man forgets what he gives and remembers what he receives. This of course, inspires him to give even more. The 24:Hour Man gives so much, he couldn't remember all he gave if he tried.

Forgiving

[98] A forgiving person is much-loved because he allows others to be themselves, which means he is vulnerable to the mistakes of others. But forgiveness acts as a shield of understanding, this allows him to easily withstand human imperfect. The 24:Hour Man is always at the ready to forgive. In fact, there's no need to ask the 24:Hour Man for forgiveness, because he can see the sorrow in your eyes. He forgives the error instantly!

Positive

[99] Whether it's his words, mood, attitude or actions the 24:Hour Man is always optimistic and encouraging. Whenever you see him you're reminded that you have a lot to be thankful for. Whenever you see him you know something good is about to happen.

Health conscious

[100] The 24:Hour Man knows that he cannot help others if he is not physically able to. He lives a healthy lifestyle: no smoking, no drug use, no high-risk activities, little or no drinking, he does not over-eat and exercises regularly.

No man is perfect

[101] A 24:Hour Man is not a perfect man, he has flaws like everyone else, but he understands that the good that he does can easily be overshadowed if he allows his imperfections to affect others. This is why he tries to keep his faults to himself. If he is a drinker, he doesn't allow his drinking to negatively affect others. If he occasionally uses harsh language, he never uses it in the presence of women or children. The 24:Hour Man knows that everything he does has consequences, so he is conscious of his every move.

> **If your actions inspire others to dream more, learn more,
> do more and become more, you are a leader.**
> John Quincy Adams

102 The 24:Hour Man knows he has a God-given job to do. What exactly is that job? Simply put, to be a giving person, 24 hours a day. He is a never-changing, ever-loving, shining example of our creator's personality. He is a consistent source of comforting love for females and a role model for boys and young men who learn from him that there is a difference between the sexes. They learn that although females may be delicate and beautiful like a flower, they are as strong and as precious as diamonds:

¹(para.65) I was finally able to silent my talkative friend with some simple logic. When I stated that a man has to put his wife's happiness above his own, he proudly and loudly stated that he had done that in the past and that he would never do it again. I said to him that if he's not going to put his wife's happiness before his own, "then why should she"? He never said another word.

²(para.66) *Instead of saying that a man is "in control" of his familial relationship, I think a better and more respectful way to put it is to say that a man is "**responsible for**" his family.*

³(para.70) *A rose bush doesn't need to be under a tree to survive, but as you can imagine, it can produce more beautiful flowers if it is protected from storms and intense heat. Likewise, a woman doesn't need the protection of a man, but when she does have protection and support she can more easily blossom into anything she wants.*

⁴(para.73) *Giving, more specifically, consistent giving, is clearly a loving act. God, his Son, and the sun are perfect examples of consistent giving. They are also perfect examples of giving without demanding repayment. Which is a good thing, because how could we pay back what God and his Son has done and continue to do for us? How can we pay back the sun? Obviously, love is not something you "pay back". To happily acknowledge what the giver has given us is the best that we can do.*

To illustrate: What if you had a job that paid you to give away money. Every day you would go to work and you would be given a thousand dollars. You would then be asked to give away $100, you can keep the rest. Would you happily acknowledge your employer and speak highly of him? Would you treat him with respect? How could you repay someone who obviously can afford anything money can buy? How can you show your appreciation for his kindness?

When you have God's love you have everything you need, what can anyone give you that's more valuable? And when you give away a little of God's love, wouldn't the receiver speak highly of you and God? And if your wife's heart is consistently overflowing with the love you give her, wouldn't she speak highly of you and treat you lovingly?

5(para.76) *Obviously, if a woman is violent or she has broken her marital vows, you have reason to leave the home. Assuming, of course, that you haven't given her a reason to be abusive or break her vows; by treating her harshly or negligently.*

6(para.82) *You received the reward of life when you woke up this morning. Having something to give is a reward. Having a giving heart is a reward. No matter how much we give, we can never give too much. It can even be said that having someone to give to is a reward, because by giving, you satisfy your natural desire to give (while also improving your ability to give). When you give to someone in need, it's as though you've parted dark clouds. And when the sun shines through, doesn't it shine on you as well?*

7(para.85) *Women who "take control of the wheel", usually do so because their husbands have let go of it. They could leap from the marriage, but many choose to lovingly steer the marriage in order to keep it from crashing. Husbands must quickly regain command, because their wives may become accustomed to being "in control". Some women may not want to relinquish control, because they may not trust that their husbands won't abandon the wheel again. So it is very important to get your finances in order as soon as possible!*

8(para.93) *Wives should be viewed the same way we view insurance; as aid that steps in temporarily in case of an emergency. The idea of living off your wife's labor should never enter your mind; just as you would never think of trying to live off chocolate cake.*

HOUR 3:
DIAMONDS AND FLOWERS

[103] **Although** diamonds are very strong that doesn't mean they are indestructible or that they don't need special care. In many ways women are like diamonds. Both are strong, but their enduring beauty is one of the characteristics that make them precious.

[104] By beauty, I'm referring to the female's femininity. It's a beauty that outshines any diamond, especially when she is properly cared for, when she is treated with love and kindness. Femininity is always as sweet as your favorite dessert, as eye pleasing as a field of daisies, and as gentle as falling snow.

[105] Once again let me state that women (no matter how strong they are), are not men and **must** be treated differently.[1] Men are like gold, they can be handled roughly and still retain their value. Women, like diamonds, don't respond well to rough treatment. A gentle touch always works best.

[106] Along with gentle treatment, a woman, like a diamond must also be protected. For example, the stone in a diamond ring, although secured by prongs, is exposed. Every woman knows to take off her rings and put them in a safe place when she is about to perform a strenuous activity. The 24:Hour Man treats his wife in a similar manner, because a wife is a man's diamond! He knows that it is his job to keep her safe, to protect her at all times and especially when things get rough.

[107] Sadly, like the man who believes that his wife's diamond ring only has value as a tool to cut glass; the man who sends his wife away to work misses out on the "real" beauty of women and many of the benefits of marriage. Like a diamond, the real beauty of a woman is what's inside, that's where the fire and passion is; a brilliance that unfortunately, goes unseen by husbands of working women.

¹⁰⁸ Diamonds, rubies, emeralds or sapphires, nothing compares to the beauty of the female. And add to that, God's most beautiful creation loves men simply because we're men, not because we're rich or handsome or tall or highly intelligent. Men (once they are financially stable) just have to be smart enough to whisper in a woman's ear that he loves her and wants to take care of her and she'll give him her heart. Of course, it takes more than words to maintain a good relationship, but sweet words will always help.

The Morning Glory

¹⁰⁹ Although women shine like diamonds, they are usually compared to flowers. They enchant us with their great variety of shapes, sizes, and colors, also because of their gentleness and delicate appearance. Women are like flowers in that they make the world more beautiful simply with their presence.

¹¹⁰ With the help of a strong support (a tree, for example), the Morning Glory brings us a bouquet of flowers every day. Together they work in complete harmony. The Morning Glory continues to produce more and more as it clings to her companion. If the tree is strong, mature, and stable it can easily support the extra weight of the flowers, while also providing an environment of protection.² Together they grow stronger and battle outside forces (heavy rain or strong winds, etc.), **not each other**!

¹¹¹ Notice the order: First, we have a strong, stable tree, **and then** the Morning Glory clings to it! Most marriages don't follow this simple pattern. In many cases, the man has not reached maturity (and financial stability), before he persuades or is persuaded by a woman to enter into a relationship. Some men quickly see they can't handle the extra weight and end the union. They then proceed to point the finger at their former wives as the main cause of the breakup, not their inability to provide for the family; the real reason for the problems in most marriages.

¹¹² Many married couples use all their energy simply trying to survive; continually overcoming issues like infidelity and money problems. Many men go into marriage like a young tree trying to bear extra weight before he has become strong enough to support it.

¹¹³ The result is that the tree (the husband) doesn't grow strong and straight. The relationship becomes twisted and loveless, and in many cases, home-life becomes worse than a war zone, fighting outside forces as well as their own partner.

¹¹⁴ God created the female to be loved and taken care of, not to be owned! In fact, you don't really **own** anything, at least not in a permanent sense. We don't even "own" our own lives. Someone or something can take it at any moment; and you certainly don't "own" a woman, no more than you can own the sun.

¹¹⁵ Females are to be admired and appreciated, and just as important, they should be loved and protected! They are to be cared for in much the same way as we care for flowers. We provide them with a safe, fertile, and loving environment. We make sure all their needs are provided. And we never expect them to do anything other than what they were designed to do. In other words, we don't expect grapes from a rose bush.

> **If a woman simply pleased my eyes like a rose,**
> **that would be more than enough.**
> T24HM!*2014

¹¹⁶ It's important that we understand that women are perfectly designed to be a complement to their husbands. They are more than qualified to assist us in any way we may need them. Their desire to please us is so strong that they often push themselves beyond their limits.

¹¹⁷ To satisfy their husbands women often attempt to do things they were not designed to do; taking the financial lead in their households, for example. This often happens when men are not financially stable when they marry. As a consequence, their wives are forced to work outside the home. They spend very little time with their husbands and therefore, have a very difficult time bonding and adapting to them.

¹¹⁸   Sadly, because working wives spend so much time working, their husbands miss out on their wives incredible ability to personalize their beauty to match their husband's desires. Women are like magical flowers that can instantly change their color, shape, and fragrance to beautify our environment.

¹¹⁹   Although women are much more than objects of great beauty, most men don't give their wives the opportunity to demonstrate their other abilities. Many wives are not in a position to show their husbands what they're capable of, because they have to spend most of their time and energy working away from home. Many men don't get the chance to see how loyal, creative, adaptable, and precious their wives are.

¹²⁰   I don't think we will ever understand the depth of a woman's love. It is as strong and as radiant as diamonds, yet as soft as rose petals.[3] Though much of their love goes unutilized, they remain ever ready to spring into action. They cry out to participate more fully in their marriages. Fortunately for men, a woman's love, like a diamond, never becomes "rusty" because of disuse. And like a rose, their love refuses to wither before the intense heat of criticism and lack of appreciation. They continue to bloom, rain or shine.

¹²¹   We have been blessed with a companion that plays her role perfectly. If more men would only realize that if they don't like what she reflects, they should change themselves or the surroundings, not the mirror. Women will just as surely reflect the good in us as the bad. A mirror has limits, it can only show us who we are. A woman can not only show us who we are, but can also help us become what we'd like to be.

¹²²   I will stress many times in this book that a man has to be financially and emotionally stable **before** he enters into a relationship; it is the only way you can provide the consistency and stability every relationship needs. You must strive to become a financially stable, 24:Hour Man, because he is more valuable than gold and stands as tall as the Mighty Oak:

¹(para.105) *One of the most important things you should learn from this book is that males and females are not the same. I was once corresponding through email with a young (22-year-old) college student and reminded him that men of high character do not use profanity, especially in the presence of females. Oddly, his response was, "Why? What makes a female any different than a male?" (I hope he wasn't studying to become a gynecologist!)*

*How sad it is that a young, college-educated man doesn't know that males and females should be treated differently. Hopefully, he will someday understand that males and females are **not** interchangeable. To this young man and others like him, I ask the question, "Where is the line?"*

By "line", I mean when should a man begin treating a female like a male? Even the crudest man has the decency to refrain from using foul language in front of young children (and most are respectful of the elderly). So then, at what age should a man begin to use profanity, for example, in the presence of females? 15? 18? 21?

*I'm sure you know the answer is never! Is a female less delicate because she's no longer a child? Is she less deserving of respect and honor because she's not a senior citizen? Just as you would never hammer a diamond, as if it were gold, you should **never** hammer a female's sensibilities with vulgar speech and crude behavior.*

²(para.110) *Where do you think you would find the most beautiful flowers, in a desert or a rainforest? Place your wife in a lush environment like a rainforest and watch the exotic beauty she produces.*

³(para.120) *In many ways women are like pillows. It is assumed that you know how to use pillows, as they don't come with instruction manuals. You know that it was designed for a specific purpose and once we find one we like, it's hard to get a good night's sleep without it.*

Like pillows, women are soft yet strong enough to support us whenever we need them. When handled properly they quickly mold themselves to us perfectly, doing so consistently and lovingly.

HOUR 4:
OAK TREES[1] AND GOLD

¹²³ **It's** easy to see that females are like flowers and should be treated gently. The rose simply blooms and it is admired for its great beauty. Plant a bulb and soon you will be rewarded with rich colors, and sweet, fresh fragrances.

¹²⁴ An oak tree, on the other hand, takes years to mature. In fact, oak trees do not produce acorns for the first 20 years of its existence. I liken men to trees, because we share similar responsibilities. An oak tree isn't planted because we want to end up with something pretty or sweet-smelling. Its looks are the least of our requirements.

¹²⁵ The uses for the oak are numerous and varied. The acorns it produces feeds animals and when acorns are planted they produce more trees. The oak tree provides shade for the very houses it was used to build. Its wood is used to make furniture and as firewood. Its branches are a sanctuary for birds, as well as a support for a child's swing. Even its bark can be used for medicinal purposes. And let's not forget all the fresh air it produces. It gives freely, asking nothing in return. The Mighty Oak **is complete as it is**! (Sound familiar?)

¹²⁶ Men, like the Mighty Oak, also have many vital responsibilities. And like the oak, if we wait until we are mature **before** we take on the responsibility of marriage and children, everyone around us will benefit. Like the oak, a man who is mature, strong, and stable (financially and emotionally) can help many people in many ways.

¹²⁷ Though men have many roles, when it comes to marriage and raising a family, being a provider is first on the list. And with his financial power the 24:Hour Man can easily fulfill his many other roles. From buying or building his home with his own two hands, to chopping the wood to heat his home, to making the furniture that furnishes it. He provides protective shade for everyone around him and fills his family's heart with love. He gives, yet asks for nothing in return, like the Mighty Oak.

Worth his weight in gold

¹²⁸ Of all the minerals mined from the earth, none is more useful than gold. Its uses are seemingly endless. Pure gold does not tarnish and it conducts electricity. It is easy to work, can be drawn into wire, can be hammered into thin sheets, alloys (blends) with many other metals and can be melted and cast into highly detailed shapes. Add to all that, it has a wonderful color and a brilliant luster.

¹²⁹ The 24:Hour Man is certainly worth his weight in gold and like the precious metal, he is also renowned for his versatility and consistency. He allows love to flow through him, he resists the corrupting influences of others and yet he's very easy to work with. Family responsibilities may spread him thin, society may hammer him, the intense heat of life's pressures may attempt to melt his very soul, but the 24:Hour Man never changes. His personality remains brilliant. His spirit consistently shines for all to see.

¹³⁰ If you compare men to gold, and women to diamonds, it's easy to understand that they are both very valuable, yet very different! Imagine the craftsmanship needed to blend them into something beautiful and lasting. To permanently attach a diamond to a gold ring takes education, patience, and focus. Marriage benefits from the same expertise.

¹³¹ Diamonds (women) that are ready to be set (married) can be attached to a ring (a man) once the ring is complete (mature and financially stable). No jeweler would attempt to attach a stone to a gold ring that wasn't finished or capable of supporting it. So again you should see the importance of a man being stable financially, spiritually, and emotionally before marriage.

¹³² But once you are financially stable and decide you would like to get married, you still need to know its rhythm and patterns, its pace and tempo, you need to learn the dance of marriage:

---

[1] (above para.123) *Oak trees are classified as members of the genus Quercus, a Latin word said to be derived from a Celtic word meaning* **"fine tree"**.

HOUR 5:

THE DANCE OF MARRIAGE

¹³³ A friend once told me that he and his wife took ballroom dance lessons and that on the first day of training, the instructor took his wife's hand and they danced around the room. What makes this significant is that she had never ballroom danced before!

¹³⁴ I called other dance schools to see if this was common. I was told that an experienced instructor could easily take an inexperienced female student and with a few quick instructions, dance around the floor with her.

¹³⁵ The interaction of a couple ballroom dancing is an almost perfect example of how marriage works. First, we have a man who has prepared himself **before** he begins the dance (of marriage). Second, we have his partner (with or without experience) who follows his lead. (Her desire to follow is much more important than her experience. As you can imagine, even if a woman had dance experience she would not be a good partner if she didn't want to follow her partner's lead.)

¹³⁶ In ballroom dancing as well as in marriage, the male dancer **has** to lead. And he has to know **how** to lead. The male dancer gently and knowingly guides his partner. Together they dance gracefully across the floor. (Could he do this without training?) He easily spins and lifts her, this won't work the other way around no matter how much training the female dancer has.

¹³⁷ Of course, there are many marriages where the female "leads", but I'm sure you know that a woman cannot work like a man and retain all her feminine qualities. Something has to be sacrificed simply because she has less time to take care of herself, to "sharpen" her feminine skills. If a woman has to take the lead, become the breadwinner, she will have to compete in a man's world, which means she may begin to behave like a man. So, unless you like "manly" women, I strongly suggest you take the lead in your marriage.

Before the dance

¹³⁸ Before you get married, even before you start a relationship, you have to know what's required to be a good husband. You must "train" to be a good husband, before you become one. Would you pay hundreds of dollars to take dance lessons from an instructor who had not finished his training? Then why get married before you know how to and are able to take care of a wife? Why would you subject a woman to months or years of missteps? (Pun intended) Reading this book is part of your training.

¹³⁹ To be a good husband and leader doesn't mean you have to know everything about relationships, just as a good dance instructor doesn't know everything about every type of dance. But a good instructor has learned the basics and continues to learn. Likewise, once you are financially stable, to be a good husband you just need to know the basics and have the desire to continue to learn more.

¹⁴⁰ But before we get on the marriage "dance floor", let me repeat once again that the most important thing you need to know to be a good husband is that you must be financially stable! Without money, even if you know all there is to know about relationships your marriage will be unstable! Why? Because knowledge doesn't pay for the never-ending necessities of life. Knowledge can't buy food, clothing, and shelter. It won't help you with those unavoidable emergencies. Knowledge pays for nothing! You need money for virtually everything. And having a little money is not good enough,[1] you must be able to completely afford the price of marriage, preferably before marriage! (No, I didn't accidentally hit copy and paste, that's a phrase I'm going to repeat over and over in this book!)

¹⁴¹ You may be a loving and understanding man. You may know the exact words to say to fill her heart with joy and you may know the perfect gifts to get her for every occasion. You can read the Bible every day and have access to all the wisdom on marriage that exists. It won't help if you don't have money. It takes money to start marriage off on the right foot and it takes money to maintain the pace, and rhythm of marriage.

¹⁴² In case you're having trouble connecting the dots, I'll make it crystal clear. The reason you must be financially stable is because you are the foundation of your marriage, not your wife. She builds her life on you. You are responsible to make sure she is safe and secure, not the other way around. She depends on you to be strong and stable. If you aren't financially stable, your marriage won't be stable!

¹⁴³ A strong and stable husband accepts full responsibility for his marriage. And just as a good dancer never blames his partner for mistakes, a good husband **never** blames his wife for problems in the marriage. **NEVER!!!** (I can't use enough exclamation points to stress how important this is. I'll explain further in Hour 8: The Blame Game.)

¹⁴⁴ I'm not saying your wife won't make mistakes, but if she's forced to do things she wasn't designed to do (like lead her household), she'll make a lot more mistakes. Imagine how confusing and stressful it must be if you are required to constantly change roles. She's expected to quickly and easily switch from being a warrior in the workplace, where she has to fiercely compete with men, then come home and be a soft, gentle loving wife and mother. (And she is punished if she mistakenly crosses those roles.) A good husband knows that it is his job to battle for his family, to lead, protect, and provide all their necessities.

¹⁴⁵ If you've seen ballroom dancing, you've probably noticed that seldom are mistakes made by the female dancer. This is remarkable when you consider that not only is she the center of attention and is much more active, she has to instantly adjust and compensate for any mistakes her partner makes. Granted, she usually reacts to her partner's lead, but she still has individual requirements that must harmonize perfectly with her partner's.

¹⁴⁶ When a man doesn't know how to lead a marriage and is not financially stable, every mistake seems huge. I've heard of couples fighting when the wife spends five dollars more than what was expected on groceries! How can a marriage be happy and stable when every penny has to be accounted for? When fights erupt when the budget is overspent by a few dollars? The answer is, it can't!

¹⁴⁷   In a nutshell, the two main reasons many marriages don't survive is because men get married broke² and don't accept the responsibility of keeping the marriage financially stable. (Many men also make their marriage even more unstable by sending their wives off to work. See Hour: 15) Most men don't know how to adjust when things don't go according to the plan they neglected to prepare. They can't fix the normal problems that arise in marriage, because they don't have the tools to fix them, namely, money and experience. Many husbands expect perfection from their mates, but expect their failure to prepare a financial plan and other shortcomings to be overlooked or understood.

¹⁴⁸   A good husband like a good dancer instructor has to know what he's doing before the dance begins! Trying to learn on the fly is not only unwise, it can also be dangerous. **After** a dancer tosses his partner in the air is not a good time to figure out how to properly catch her. If you want your wife to give you her complete trust and faith, she has to be sure not only that you know how to catch her, but also that you are capable of catching her. She can't catch herself!

¹⁴⁹   Even a good leader makes mistakes, some things are simply unavoidable. But if he trips, it will not be because he is unprepared or careless or selfish. A good leader prepares for problems and is quick to resolve them. He learns from his mistakes and if he should fall, it won't be long before he's back on his feet.

¹⁵⁰   Because women are more emotional they sometimes blame their husbands for problems in their marriage. But when problems spring up, she shouldn't be faulted for stating the obvious. As the leader of your family, you have to accept the fact that everything falls on you. A little complaining from your wife should mean nothing more to you than a reminder that she needs to be comforted and reassured. (For everything a woman "nags" about, there are probably 10 things she ignores!) Her complaining is a clear signal that she feels insecure, it's your job to quickly make her feel safe.

[151] Once again, before you begin the dance of marriage, you must be financially stable. Money equals power and with it, you are prepared to battle almost any problem and keep your family safe! When problems arise your partner will follow your confident lead and calmly assist you in any way you need.

[152] If you prepare yourself before marriage, you can adjust to almost anything this life may throw at you. But a man with little or no money is forced to stumble along trying to learn the dance of marriage one step at a time. He will feel unsure of every decision he makes, of every step he takes, as though he's walking on a wobbly tightrope:

[1] *(para.140) This is one of those confusing, problem areas for men who can't figure out why their relationship is not working although they are "contributing". When a woman gets involved with a man she expects him to be a man in every sense of the word, 100% of the time. Women want 24:Hour Men, a man who is complete. A man who can fully take care of all her needs, not "contribute" to her needs. This is what women assume when they enter into a relationship with a man. Just as men assume that their wives will remain sweet, feminine, and loving. Wouldn't you find it odd (and disturbing), if one day your wife wore a beautiful, lacy dress and the next day, for no apparent reason, she wore a man's suit, along with a man's hat and shoes! Just as you expect her to remain feminine, she expects you to consistently provide traditional male traits.*

"Contributing" financially to a relationship is only slightly better than giving nothing. For example, what if you had an emergency and needed a thousand dollars. You need the money because you are scheduled to be evicted from your home the following day. A friend calls and tells you he will rush over the next day and give you all the money you need. But when he arrives the following day, he only has $200! Would you show appreciation for his "contribution"? Of course not! Had you not relied on his word you may have been able to find another avenue of assistance. At this point his contribution is actually worse than nothing!

Women love men and marriage. They happily jump hand in hand with the man they love into the deep end of the pool, only to find out, often times, that their man can't swim. This is the situation many women find themselves. Relying on men who cannot produce as promised. Had she not relied on the financially unstable man's word she could have sought out a mate that could actually provide for her and her children (financially and emotionally). Instead, she is forced to do things she was not designed to do (like working outside the home) and she has to "contribute" in ways she did not expect.

[2] *(para.147) When I use the word "broke", I don't necessarily mean penniless. Although, as you just read in the previous footnote, there isn't much difference between a man who has no money and a man who doesn't have "enough" money, especially when it comes to keeping a household running smoothly.*

HOUR 6:
TIGHTROPE WALKER

¹⁵³ **If** you want to have a successful marriage, it's best to start it on stable (financial) ground. But many people believe it's best to struggle together, because they think it will make the relationship grow stronger. Although this notion has been romanticized in movies and on television, **it is the absolute worst way to start a marriage**! Indeed, some marriages make it through tough times, but memories of suffering remain in your mind forever! Memories of pain and struggle are ugly and permanent![1]

¹⁵⁴ Wouldn't you rather look back on good memories, like the time you surprised your wife with a trip to Hawaii? Or the "romantic" time you spent the night sleeping in your car, because you were kicked out of your apartment. How about the time she spent all day shopping for the ingredients for a special candlelight dinner. Or the "fun" time you had warming up the last can of Beanee Weenee with a candle, because that was all you had to eat and the electricity was shut off?

¹⁵⁵ Just in case I'm being too subtle, the point I'm trying to get across, once again, is that you must be financially stable **before you even consider marriage**!

A financially unstable marriage feels as "secure" as walking a shaky tightrope without a safety net!

¹⁵⁶ Imagine a tightrope walker walking on a tightrope. I'm sure you've seen this many times. The funambulist expertly jumps, dances, spins, and even pretends to fall! He can be as "reckless" and daring as he wants, because he's only responsible for himself. (And he was highly trained **before** he stepped onto the rope.)

¹⁵⁷ Now imagine an untrained tightrope walker walking the rope blindfolded, with his wife on his back! Do you think he can do any of those tricks? This is how many marriages begin; with an inexperienced, financially unstable man attempting to reach the stable end of a wobbly rope, while carrying his wife (and sometimes kids) on his back. A very difficult feat even with training!

¹⁵⁸ Walking in the darkness of the blindfold makes the rope seem endless (without a financial plan, it seems the bad times will never end). Every step is a struggle (every day is stressful). No fancy tricks, every inch is measured (no surprises, every penny has to be accounted for). There is no cheering audience, in fact, they jeer your pathetic performance (friends offer little or no support, in fact, they often suggest you divorce).

¹⁵⁹ The absolute assurance of daily strife and combat with your mate forces many couples to seek the "relief" of divorce. For many others, the husband decides he can't carry (support) his wife and sends her off to work, if she isn't already working. He reasons that it will make things easier. In the beginning, he may be relieved of a little pressure, but (there's always a "but") now the marriage is exposed like an open wound. By making things easier on himself, he has made things infinitely more difficult for his wife! (As you shall see in Hour: 15)

No Teamwork!

¹⁶⁰ When a wife is forced to work away from home the team is now split, because the couple is walking the wobbly rope independently. Things may go smoothly in the beginning, but with their newfound "freedom", they are more impulsive and less careful and considerate. Because they are now leading separate lives, it is very difficult to stay coordinated! They find themselves doing the things they did when they were single, because that's how they feel. Their independent movements will cause the rope to shake more wildly and uncontrollably than ever.

¹⁶¹ By making things "easier", the couple (actually, the financially unstable husband) has unwittingly made their marriage feel even more unsafe and unstable. Because they have so little time to spend with each other, they don't have the option of clinging to each other to get a sense of security and oneness. Many will then reach for anything (drugs or alcohol) or anyone that promises "security" or "comfort". Because of our natural desire for affection and attention, it won't be long before "comfort" comes in the form of another man or woman, suddenly the team has new players!

¹⁶² Some may argue that you can get across the tightrope (struggle together) by walking slowly and being careful. This may be true, but there

are outside forces working against marriage. If the rope remained perfectly still, you could get through life, inch by inch, simply trying to survive; never doing anything other than working, eating, and sleeping. In other words, not only would you have to follow the plan perfectly (which is virtually impossible considering life's normal ups and downs), but you would have to live a very boring, monotonous, and fearful life, possibly forever.

163   I'm sure you've seen marriages like this; couples that focus all their energy on working and paying bills, the "Roommate" marriage. If that's the kind of marriage you want, by all means, have at it.

164   No matter what type of marriage you have, when you start a marriage without financial stability someone or something is going to be there to "shake the rope". Trouble is never far off. Even small things can cause big problems. When the rope starts to sway and fear sets in, invariably the couple will begin to fight each other, not what's causing the rope to tremble! And the more they fight, the more unstable the marriage will become.

165   The wife blames her husband for placing her (and in many cases, their children) in such a dangerous situation and the husband blames his "emotional" wife for panicking and making things worse. Isn't it funny how emotional a woman can be when her family is in danger or when she is about to be homeless or when she finds lipstick on her husband's collar? (Add sarcasm here.)

166   Financially unstable couples can very easily and quickly be torn apart when they both work outside the home, because they are no longer a team. They are just two fearful, confused people on a wobbly rope; married, but feeling single and alone. The marriage is being held together by reasons other than love and devotion: the kids, tax purposes, nowhere else to go. It seems so much easier to jump into the arms of anyone offering support. (And very often that's what happens.)

167   When most people look back on the hard times and laugh, they usually look back alone, because they're now divorced! The idea that struggling will strengthen a marriage is a lie! Struggling adds **nothing positive** to marriage. Instead, it adds doubt, insecurity, turmoil, tension and stress (and that's the short list).

¹⁶⁸ Couples that somehow manage to survive the years of struggle are rewarded for their efforts with spine-chilling, frightful memories that never go away. They have many shocking images burned into their minds like scenes from a horror film that they starred in. These terrible memories often resurface for various reasons. They are easily triggered and can even haunt them in their dreams. They unpredictably spook them like a reoccurring nightmare!

¹⁶⁹ Here's the chorus once again. If a man prepares himself, by working hard to become financially stable **before** he gets married, his marriage will be a lot more stable and manageable. You must be prepared to tackle what many people say is the biggest problem most marriages face, lack of money:

---

¹(para.153) *We all know couples who have stayed together after enduring years of struggle. But in many cases, the length of a marriage has nothing to do with the quality of the marriage. I have heard tragic stories of struggle that brought tears to my eyes just listening to them. Most of the chaos was caused by money problems. Struggling has by no means made their marriage stronger!*

The idea that struggling can make a marriage stronger makes about as much sense as a sprinter thinking he can improve his speed and technique by running on a wet track full of potholes and rocks, during a sandstorm! When the training is over, his damaged body will show the bruises of this insane training method. The sight of his permanently scarred body will be a constant reminder of the pain he endured.

HOUR 7:
MONEY COMMA, EVERYTHING ELSE[1]

170   A man may be fantastic in every way: smart, caring, generous, etc. But if he doesn't have enough money to fully support his family, his marriage will eventually become just as unstable as the man who is dull, selfish, and inconsiderate. Any man contemplating marriage **has** to be financially stable and **then** he can work on everything else.

171   As you've noticed throughout this book, I've stressed (and will continue to stress) the importance of a man being financially stable **before** marriage. If you enter into a marriage financially unstable not only will you struggle emotionally and physically, but you and your mate will rarely have that feeling of security and calmness. Like a mountain climber with no lifeline or the driver of a car with damaged brakes or a man walking a wobbly tightrope with no safety net, you will seldom feel at ease. I don't want the idea of you entering into a relationship financially unprepared to even cross your mind. It is a nonnegotiable point that I will make over and over in this book!

172   To make the title of this hour a little clearer, imagine a woman preparing to bake a pie.[2] She has gathered the best and freshest ingredients she can find. But after mixing all the ingredients, she won't be able to finish unless she has the most important part, the crust. Every pie is different, but every pie has a crust. Likewise, every man has his own "ingredients", but when it comes to marriage, every husband should have one thing in common, money, financial stability. Financial stability is the "crust" that men fill with their "ingredients": generosity, concern for others, patience, etc.

173   To use a restaurant analogy, what rating would you give a fancy eatery if the food was horrible? Would the ambiance matter? What if the prices were reasonable and the wait staff was very friendly and professional? Obviously, the food is the first (and in many cases the only) thing that persuades a customer to return. (The best taco I ever had was from a gas station!) Nothing else matters if the food is bad! In other words, the first thing a restaurant must have is good food and **then** it can work on everything else.

174 Many people I talk to about relationships often come away thinking that I believe money will solve all marital problems and that you can't have a successful marriage without money. The fact of the matter is they're half right, I don't believe in the vast majority of cases you can have a happy, healthy marriage without money. On the other hand, I don't believe money is a cure-all.

175 A lack of money will destroy a marriage almost 100% of the time or at the very least, turn it into something ugly. The reason I stress the importance of money, is because men that don't have enough money to support their families are not happy. A man may be perfect in every other respect, but if he can't take care of his family guilt will begin to eat away his soul, leaving an empty, sad, confused, bitter man. Feeling inadequate is devastating to men. To ease the pain many men turn to alcohol or drugs or women, this of course will make matters much worse.

176 On the other hand, having money, being financially stable doesn't guarantee that you'll have a good marriage, just as having an umbrella on a rainy day won't guarantee you won't get wet. There have been occasions when I've been caught in bad weather and even though I had an umbrella, most of my body still got soaked! But regardless of my past experiences I would never go out into bad weather without an umbrella. Just as an umbrella won't guarantee you won't get wet, financial stability won't guarantee a happy successful marriage, but it increases the odds substantially!

177 And to take the umbrella analogy one step further, it's wise to purchase an umbrella before you need one. In case you've somehow missed the point I've stated several times, it's best to be financially stable **before** you get married. It becomes increasingly more difficult to do so after you get married. (Recall Hour: 6 Tightrope Walker) Just as it is best to get health insurance before you need it, as it is virtually impossible to get properly insured after you get sick without paying outrageously high premiums!

178 So once again, if you want to have a happy, stable marriage you will absolutely need to be financially stable. This is a very simple rule that you must follow. It's a rule that women understand, although they don't always follow it. Women may not always respect and understand men, but all women respect and understand that money equals stability. They understand that money can take care of most of their needs and it can be used for protection. Money never changes, in other words, it's consistent, just like a 24:Hour Man.

Love is blind and often broke[3]

179 Women, not wanting to appear materialistic (plus a strong desire to love and be loved), often marry men with little or no money. They have the belief that love will conquer all. Love may indeed conquer all, but it'll take a terrible beating in the process! Love's power often blinds women to the fact that a man who is not financially stable is not a pleasant creature to be married to. Many of love's promises are soon broken, mainly because of a lack of finances. In most marriages, hope (and a little love) is all that's left. Things may somehow get better, but in the meantime, she'd better hold onto her hat, because she may be in for a long, bumpy ride!

180 Oddly, one of the biggest problems most marriages face--lack of money, should be one of the easiest to overcome. I say that because it's a problem you both see. You know how much money you have in your bank account. Bills don't sneak up on you. You know what the problem is and you know how to fix it; make more money and/or live a simpler lifestyle. But there are several reasons why this enemy (lack of money) destroys so many marriages.

181 Getting married with little or no money causes your marriage to be on shaky ground from the start. Your new wife, who wants to be your cheerleader, must now enter the game and battle with you. You have little or no time to bond and consequently, you don't. A lack of money often shows itself from the start when a man isn't able to pay for his own wedding and many can't pay for the rings!

182 The honeymoon period is very short and instead of focusing on the marriage, paying bills immediately becomes the top (and soon, the only) priority. The blushing bride soon becomes the boisterous bride, because her dreams have quickly been shattered. I'm not attacking the good intentions of men. I'm simply stating that lots of men get married before they are financially stable and don't seem to know why their marriage is so rocky.

¹⁸³ The lack of a plan, a team plan, is another reason many marriages struggle to survive. Let's not forget what marriage means. Marriage is the union of a man and woman as husband and wife, with common goals and an understanding of their roles. To reach those goals it helps if each partner knows what the goals are and what the plan is.

¹⁸⁴ The normal flow of marriage should be very simple; the husband goes to work for 8 hours and comes home to his wife. But when you start a marriage in a financial hole, the "normal" course of marriage becomes: the husband goes to work for 8 or more hours, the wife goes to work for 8 or more hours (sometimes pregnant). The husband comes home to rest. The wife comes home to begin her next job, housework. The house needs to be cleaned, she cleans it. Dinner needs to be prepared, she cooks it. The kids need to be taken care of, she cares for them. The exhausted wife prepares to do the same thing again tomorrow and goes to bed. The husband wants his exhausted wife to take care of his sexual needs, the "other woman" takes care of it. The wife catches her husband with the other woman. The husband blames his wife for not taking care of his needs!

¹⁸⁵ A new enemy has attacked the marriage, infidelity (that means cheating). The rocky marriage has now become rockier. Verbal and physical abuse will soon be added to the mix. This doesn't sound like marital bliss to me, but many people think that a normal marriage consists of battling issue after issue, while also violently battling each other. Predictably, as long as money problems exist, trouble and chaos will be a part of what many consider a normal marriage. What later follows is also what society has come to call normal, 911 calls, separation, and divorce.

¹⁸⁶ Financial problems, if not resolved quickly, **will** destroy most marriages (or turn it into something freakish; like "open marriages" and couples living in separate homes). Many men see the problems that lack of money creates and over compensate by working extra hours[4] (or even worse, sending their wives out to work). Unfortunately, the well-intentioned plan of working more will also put stress on the marriage, because now the wife rarely has her husband around to bond with, to stay bonded to. And she will also have to assume more of her husband's normal duties and still maintain hers. It seems every move you make is wrong when you enter marriage financially unprepared.

Money gives you options[5]

187   Money isn't the only thing you need to have a successful marriage, but it is the **first** thing you'll need. (I'm assuming, of course, that you have physical and emotional attraction.) Having money doesn't mean you won't have challenges. There will always be necessities, bills, and unexpected expenses. Money is an essential tool to help marriage run smoother. It's a tool married men use to take care of their wives, who in turn will then take care of their husbands. That's a simple and easy to follow pattern.

188   Financially stable men are confident and like to do things themselves. If they have marital problems, they honestly believe they can fix them. Some are able to, but others realize they need help and because they have money, they can seek other options. One of those options, although I don't recommend it, is marriage counseling.

189   Most marriage counselors will tell you that money won't solve problems and in the next breath tell you that 90% of divorces are caused by money problems![6] All the while, charging you hundreds of dollars, thereby making your money problems worse! Counseling (even if it's free), like many relationship books, often does more harm than good, as it rarely gets to the actual problem. (Lack of money, in most cases.) For most couples, all the "marital counseling" you need can be found in this book.

190   Money won't solve every problem you may face, but it will at least give you more options to help settle problems. To put it simply, money equals options, little or no money equals few or no options. A man (or woman) who feels he has no options feels helpless and desperate. A desperate man is more easily tempted to get involved in illegal or risky activities in an effort to make money. This will of course lead to other problems.

191   I believe money (when used properly), combined with a loving attitude, can solve most marital problems. This is a simple solution that many people think is too simple. But if, for example, you want to keep your car running smoothly, you don't paint it or buy expensive rims, you simply make sure it has enough oil. In other words, if you give a marriage what it needs, it **will**

run smoothly. The only thing that most struggling couples need is for the husband to make more money (and of course, use that money to take care of his family). This will lead to him feeling and acting more confidently.

¹⁹² A man has to feel confident in his ability to take care of his family and the only thing that will make him feel confident, **consistently**, is money. Financial stability is particularly important during the early period of a relationship that is headed toward marriage. This is when most adjustments are made and this is when a man can show he is able to make use of money's primary option, that of being a provider.

¹⁹³ Although this hour is called "Money Comma, Everything Else", the "everything else" is important also as it includes the way a man speaks to his wife. Speaking to your wife in a harsh, demeaning, accusatory tone will not help her bond to you, no matter how much money you have. In the next hour we're going to play a dangerous game. You're going to need a good bat, because I'm going to throw you a curveball. We're going to play the Blame Game:

[1] (Above para.170) *Ecclesiastes 7:12 – "For wisdom is a defense, and money is a defense." I have debated many men about the importance of money in marriage. Many have stated that marriages don't fail because of money. The fact of the matter is that they are partially correct. Money or lack of money is not what causes most marriages to fall apart. It is the lack of defense or protection that money provides that exposes marriage to everything that can and **will** attack it.*

When a marriage is faced with money problems, its defenses are completely stripped away, it is similar to contracting AIDS. Like the AIDS virus, the "lack-of-money" virus causes the condition of the "infected" marriage to get progressively worse. And when Love, the last line of defense is attacked, the couple will turn on each other and destroy the marriage.

Fortunately, you can cure this "disease" by building a strong financial "immune system". You can restore the health of your marriage by making more money (or living a simpler lifestyle), and using its power to make sure your wife always feels safe and loved.

[2] *(para.172) Even when it comes to baking a pie, the baker knows that it's best to have all the necessary ingredients **before** you get started. Marriage deserves (requires) just as much forethought and preparation. The idea of being prepared is plainly expounded in Luke 14:28 – "But **don't begin** until you count the cost. For who would begin construction of a building without **first** calculating the cost to see if there is enough money to finish it?" (Emphasis mine)*

Here's another example of what I mean by Money Comma, Everything Else: Imagine you have a car for sale and a prospective buyer wants to come to your home to discuss the details of a cash transaction. When he arrives he begins to tell you about his good driving record and that he has never had an accident. He says he is a mechanic and is also good at detailing cars. He shows you pictures of his wife and kids, and explains how your car would make an excellent family car. He even tells you that he has a good job and has good credit.

It won't be long before this "idle" chitchat causes you to yell, "Show me the money!" None of these minor details will get his name on the title. The only thing that's going to stop his friendly words from quickly exiting your good ear is when he plugs it with cold cash. Until he starts talking about money, nothing else matters! Likewise, it doesn't matter if you're the most caring, honest, religious man who ever lived, until you get your finances in order, nothing you can do will keep your marriage stable.

[3] *(above para.179) Love, loves love more than anything else. Love doesn't care who it loves, it wants your undying devotion, yet it is jealous. Love seems to stay only as long as you love it. It sometimes seems hard to find, but it's never far away.*

Women love love, even though it's an insatiable, mysterious force. It frightens some men, but no woman seems to fear it. It has many forms and is sometimes unrecognizable. It holds you tight, but never lets you have control of it. It knows what you're thinking and anticipates your every move.

Women love love, and can't understand why men don't seem to love love too. Women appear to have influence over this spirit, but not complete. So be advised to keep her happy, for fear she may not let love loose. Love hurts because it wants to be set free. Like the burning in your chest when you hold your breath, love won't come in until you let love out.

The reason that I wax poetic is to show you that women and love are a package and they are not to be played with. You can't have one without the other; no more than you can have her body without her heart. In time she may blend her love with yours, but know that you can't take back that love without consequences. As long as you keep her secure you'll see that the only thing women love more than love, is you.

[4] *(para.186) Working more hours is probably the best plan of action until a better option can be found. Make sure your wife knows what the plan is and what the goals are. In the meantime, pay special attention to Hour: 18.*

[5] *(above para.187) One simple option that money affords when marriage gets a little shaky is to pay for a "mini vacation" from each other. Go to a hotel for a day or visit a family member. Give yourself time to cool off. And while you're away concentrate on Hour: 21, 4 Powerful Relationship Strengthening Techniques.*

[6] *(para.189) I don't want to get involved in predicting divorce, as many people stay together for years, though you would not describe their marriage as blissful. But I can certainly state that if you have money problems, your marriage will have far more bad times than good.*

HOUR 8:

THE BLAME GAME

¹⁹⁴ In my opinion, blaming can be as deadly to a marriage (or any type of relationship) as money problems. As stated in Hour 7, money problems are out in the open, you can see them. More importantly, money problems can often be corrected quickly with teamwork. By simply taking care of your wife's basic needs and making sure she doesn't have to work outside the home, married life can be enjoyable. If a couple works together, they can successfully overcome almost any problem.

¹⁹⁵ Until you reach financial stability, be careful not to make the journey more stressful with hurtful comments. Blaming makes it difficult for couples to work together, because they are attacking each other with painful, biting words. When a man blames his wife for marital problems he will damage his marriage, whether he's justified or not (even if he's financially stable).

A good leader never blames others, he accepts the blame

¹⁹⁶ A good leader, a good husband, protects, and loves his wife and when things go wrong he accepts the blame, even if it's not his fault! A good leader is caring, patient, and understands that no one is perfect. A good husband knows and appreciates the many differences between men and women. He knows that a woman who always feels safe, always feels loved and she will reflect the love she receives. He understands that if his wife is not satisfying his needs, there's probably a good reason why; maybe it's because he's not satisfying hers. Whatever the problem, a good leader takes it upon himself to solve it.

¹⁹⁷ Blaming is an extremely dangerous weapon and some men have taken it to an even lower level by blaming others for mistakes **they** commit. Recall what you read in Hour 7 (para.184), "The husband blames his wife for not taking care of his needs." (Here comes the curveball.) Many of the negative statements men make about their wives are true! Some wives don't take care of their husband's needs. But remember that wives are a reflection of their husbands. Therefore, if a wife is not taking care of the needs of her husband, you can almost guarantee that he has not taken care of hers.

It's Alive!

198 Many men tell me horror stories about their wives; how they have been neglected and tormented, and that their wives (and ex-wives) are monsters. I tell them that I agree that what has happened to them is terrible and that if what they say is true, then maybe they are married to monsters! I then tell them to warn the villagers, because the monster **they've** created is loose and no one is safe!

199 If you think your wife is a monster, then you must be Doctor Frankenstein, because surely an intelligent man would never have married such a terrible creature. (Cue the violins and insert sarcasm.) I'm sorry that you've had to suffer so much considering all the hard work you've put into your marriage.

200 Surely you must have seen this coming; after all, she is your creation! A monster created by years of mistreatment and neglect, and brought to life by the shocking realization that she has wasted the best years of her life on someone who doesn't love or appreciate her.

201 The point I am trying not so subtly to make is that if you don't treat a woman with love and tenderness (and above all, keep her safe), the result will often be the creation of a "monster": a mean, bitter, distrustful, and vengeful woman. A person who has had her soul ripped out. Not by society, who she expects to be uncaring at times, but by the person she has opened herself up to and who she expects to love, and protect her.

202 Instead, she has no protection, no love, and seemingly nowhere to turn. And to make matters worse, she is then "blamed" for being the very thing she was created to be; a part-man, part-woman, freak of nature. She is forced to work long and hard like a man; cook, clean, and have sex like a woman, and sit quietly in a closet like a machine until needed. (I'll stop here before I go into full "male-bashing" mode.)

203 A bad leader/husband uses flawed logic and thinks to himself, "I work 8 hours and come home. I am a little tired, but not too tired to have sex. I want my needs met. My wife also works 8 hours and comes home. And like me, she shouldn't be too tired to have sex, because she's a human like I am.

But for some strange reason, after taking care of the kids, cooking dinner, cleaning the house, repairing the roof, and mowing the lawn she won't take care of my needs. Something must be wrong with her!"

204 The trap is now set by twisted logic. If she doesn't satisfy her husband's needs, (in his mind) he can justify cheating by blaming his wife for not performing her "duties". (Overlooking the fact that he hasn't performed his duty of making sure his wife is safe and doesn't have to work outside the home.) But if she continues to push her body, it's only a matter of time before she breaks down.

205 And when she breaks down and **can't** take care of her "duties", we're right back where we started; the husband not being satisfied and then blaming his wife for not taking care of his needs. Many men follow this type of illogical thinking, therefore, for those men, please pay special attention to the following message:

Men and women are not the same!

206 In case you hadn't noticed, women are those humans that are usually smaller, softer, and gentler than other humans. Many of them wear dresses, and jewelry, makeup and perfume. Though they look similar to men, they're not!

207 A sure way to end a marriage is to treat a woman like a man and become proficient at the blame game.[1] The role of a wife can be very demanding (especially if she's married to a financially unstable man), but expecting a woman to perform like a man and then ripping her when she makes a mistake is borderline abusive.

208 I'm sure you've heard the business edict, "The customer is always right". I think this should be changed to, "The customer's always right, even when they're wrong". This leads me to the 24:Hour Man's marital decree:

A wife is never blamed, even when she makes a mistake!

209 The "customer is always right", business adage is used so that customers will always think that their needs will be quickly taken care of; that

they are appreciated and very important. Your wife should have that same guarantee of "customer satisfaction", that same assurance. A good manager immediately tries to find a solution to a customer's problem. A good husband, in like manner, should immediately try to fix any problem his marriage may face, not affix blame, no matter who or what caused the problem!

210   Does blaming or berating a person for a mistake create a positive, calm atmosphere? Does blaming bring about anything positive? Don't forget you're not dealing with a man. Men normally have thick skin and can accept a little criticism. But some men treat women worse than men, using loud, abusive language, and even name-calling, taking the blame game to yet another level.

211   If you want a happy marriage, **remember to fight the problem**, not your mate! Blaming others implies that you never make mistakes or that your mistakes are not as bad and therefore should be ignored. If you blame your wife for a mistake she's made, the mistake still exists, but now you have an unhappy partner who may not help you fix the problem. So why waste time and energy blaming, arguing, and fault-finding, **FIX THE PROBLEM!**

> **Be not angry that you cannot make others as you wish them, since you cannot even make yourself as you wish to be.**
> T. A. Kempkis

212   While money problems and blaming hurt many marriages, they are just a couple of its enemies. Lots of mistaken ideas about marriage and relationships keep them from becoming solid. One is the belief that all marital responsibilities should be split down the middle, as if men and women are interchangeable and have the same skills and abilities. This is another example of men treating women like men. I call this the 50-50 myth:

[1]*(para.207) A controversial radio personality often refers to women, and especially wives, as "dream killers". He states that once a man gets married he has to stop reaching for his dreams. He uses twisted logic and blames women for a man's decision to get married before he is financially stable. This is a perfect example of blaming others for your choices.*

HOUR 9:
MYTH BUSTING

213 **There** are many myths about marriage that keep couples off-balance. Oddly, one of them is called the 50/50 theory; we both work, we split the bills, she buys her wedding ring and I buy mine. Everything is split down the middle. I say oddly, because on the surface, this seems fair. But, once again, men and women aren't the same and don't have the same responsibilities when it comes to marriage.

214 This type of marriage will slowly become weak and eventually die, because the only things that are usually split are the financial responsibilities. Wives are still required to maintain their "duties" (cooking, cleaning, tending to children, etc.) at peak performance!

215 It amazes me when I hear a 6'4" man say he can't understand why his 5'4" wife is always tired after working a few hours and taking care of a few kids. He doesn't seem to realize that the female body is simply not designed to work 8 or more hours a day (sometimes while pregnant), then rush home to do the laundry, take care of kids, cook, clean the house, shop, run errands, and do yard work. This leaves her about 10 minutes to eat, bathe, and spend time with her husband.

216 Why is it that men can be completely understanding when it comes to the limitations of a highly trained, well-conditioned professional athlete, but are completely perplexed as to why their wives have limitations? For example, the center on a basketball team is not expected to be a good dribbler or jump shooter, but when it comes to wives, they are expected to do everything a man can do, without complaining or getting tired or making mistakes. They are expected to be great shooters, rebounders, defenders, and passers. They must supply the towels and water during timeouts, be a cheerleader at halftime and of course, always make the game winning shot! (All for no pay and no guaranteed contract!)

217 Wives should be given the same understanding as the athlete. Actually, your wife should receive more understanding, because she is the one you vowed to love and take care of. She is the one you promised to make the game winning shot for!

218   Just because a woman is willing to do whatever she can to keep her family together doesn't mean she can handle it. Besides, if you really want to have a marriage where everything is split down the middle, a woman should be allowed to say to her husband, "Dear, I had the last baby, now it's your turn." But of course, your wife does understand your limitations and would never ask this of you; so let's comprise. She'll have the baby and you watch it while she plays golf.

219   One thing you should learn from this hour is that the 24:Hour Man doesn't need anyone to help him pay half the bills; he takes the responsibility of paying all of them, just like he did before he got married.

220   He knows that if he chooses to get married, it is his job to take care of all his wife's needs and that anything she brings to his life is a bonus. He knows that a wife is a blessing, perfectly designed to assist him. He knows that the only way his wife can properly do her "job" of assisting him, is if he does his job of fully supporting her.

221   He understands that his wife should work outside the home **only in extreme cases!** And if a situation arises that makes it necessary for his wife to get a job, he does everything he can to quickly get back on his feet so that his wife can return to the safety of her home. Let me stress, if a married woman has to work outside the home it should be understood by all that it is only for a short time! (I think this is a good place for an analogy.) If you were to break your leg, you would need crutches only for a short time, until you get back on your feet, not for the rest of your life!

222   Your wife already has many important jobs to do. The most important, after taking care of herself, is taking care of you! She can't assist you if she has to focus all her time and energy on other things. But if you insist on things being 50/50, then allow your wife to spend half her time caring for herself and the other half caring for you.

Bad boys, are just **boys** who are bad!

223   Another myth is that women like "bad boys". (A better description would be "rotten boys".)[1] Regardless of what some women say, all women like men who have good character and who are in control of their lives.[2] Some may also like a little ruggedness, for men to be a little rough around the edges, but there's a big difference between rugged and rotten.

224 The image of the "bad boy" is of a rough and tough, manly man. I hesitate to use the word "manly" when referring to rotten boys, because to be manly means to be courageous and brave. Other synonyms include: noble, chivalrous, dignified, and valiant. Those words don't describe rotten boys, but they do describe the 24:Hour Man!

225 Rotten boys get attention because it's easy to be bad. It's easier to take or steal, than to work. They're loud and aggressive, and plentiful, like roaches. Rotten boys are like cheap fast food; actually, they're worse than fast food. They're more like a hot dog that's been sitting on the grill all day. Someone buys it just before it's thrown into the garbage.

226 Bad boys are leeches that suck the life out of women, leaving nothing but an empty body that no man would want, except, of course, another bad boy. Bad boys are worthless men who do nothing but take! They circle the skies like vultures looking for lonely women, especially women with money.

227 They can always find a woman to latch onto because they know women like men who **appear** manly and offer, at least temporarily, some form of affection and comfort. I must admit also that some rotten boys do offer a little protection for women as they are often armed and aggressive. But this protection, of course, is relative, as women will very often find themselves needing protection from the rotten boy!

228 Even women who claim they like bad boys are referring to the "good" side of the bad boy. I'm sure they don't like being cheated on, stolen from or used as punching bags, which is what bad boys do. They think that they can have a good relationship with a bad boy if only he would be good consistently.[3] In other words, what they really want are 24:Hour Men, because if rotten boys were good consistently they wouldn't be rotten boys!

229 Rotten boys are almost always single, which makes it easier for them to jump from woman to woman. Rotten boys swarm like mosquitoes, attacking at every angle. Most women are too busy swatting these pests away to even notice a good man if he walked by. (Unfortunately, the odds of these women finding a good man are low, because good men don't like women who associate with worthless men.)

230   If single women were given the opportunity to spend time with a group of eligible businessmen or a group of rotten boys, the vast majority would choose the group of businessmen. Unfortunately, women aren't usually given this choice, so they begin to believe there are no good men available. They then find themselves involved with the scum under the rock they've inadvertently kicked over.

> **A bad boy is just a shell of a <u>real</u> man;
> A man <u>only</u> on the outside.**
> T24HM!*2014

231   Sadly, women often choose rotten boys simply because there are so many of them;[4] just as there are many more fast food joints than 5-star restaurants. But where do you think a woman would choose to eat if she had the choice? I'm sure you know the answer. And I'm sure a woman would choose to spend time with a 24:Hour Man if she could find one.

232   Many women believe there are very few men who would make good husbands. This myth does have some truth to it. Although there are plenty of good men, being a good man doesn't mean he'll be a good husband. (And worthless, bad boys certainly don't make good husbands!) Hopefully, you should see by now that a man can't be a good husband unless he's financially stable. So, instead of simply looking for a good man, I believe a woman should look for a good, financially stable man.[5]

233   A good husband is not a myth. There are many of them, but there are a lot more bad ones. And there is a large group of men who simply don't know how to be good husbands, primarily, because they were not raised by one. Hopefully, after reading this book we will have more good men for women to choose from. Men who know they are fully responsible to take care of the financial and emotional needs of their families. More men who treat women like women, not like men and who respect and appreciate the many talents of women. Men who understand that if they treat their wives with love and kindness, they will remain as beautiful (inside and out) as the day they met.

234   If you're still having trouble understanding how a 24:Hour Man should treat a woman, let's go to the farm and get our hands dirty:

[1] (para.223) What makes having a good relationship with a rotten boy even more difficult and ill-advised is the fact that most of them were not raised by their fathers. This means they have absolutely no idea how a good relationship is supposed to function! They don't have a clue how to properly treat women and believe violence is normal. Some don't even realize they are doing anything unusual or wrong. They don't understand what it means to sacrifice or how to put the needs of others before their own.

[2] (para.223) I was going to write "**good** women, like men who have good character", but this would imply that many women are inherently bad. We are in many cases a product of our environment, therefore, our treatment and understanding of women should be based on how she was raised; whether or not she was taken care of as a child and how she may have been treated in a previous relationship. For example, if you were looking to buy a large mirror, you know that the mirrors on the showroom floor are usually well taken care of (dusted, polished, etc.). But the mirrors kept in the back stockroom may not have received proper care. Many of them may have frames that are scratched or chipped. If you were to purchase a mirror that has been kept in the stockroom, it may need to be restored, which takes time and special attention. You wouldn't look at a mirror from the stockroom as being "bad" or "good", simply cared for or not cared for and you would treat it accordingly.

A similar example would be restoring classic cars. If you found a 57' Chevy that had been sitting in a garage for years, you wouldn't look at it as "good or bad", simply in need of care. But unlike classic cars, women don't need anyone to "restore" them. Women who live in a loving environment and are fully supported, can quickly and easily "restore" themselves.

[3] (para.228) Many women believe that if they love a bad boy, he will "reflect" love in return. It should be obvious that this plan won't work, because bad boys are takers and have no desire to give anything, especially not love, at least not on a consistent basis. Trying to extract consistent love from a rotten, bad boy is as impossible as drinking muddy, sea water and believing you can spit out the salt and dirt!

[4] (para.231) *Some women with drug or alcohol problems may prefer the company of bad boys, because most bad boys also have drug and alcohol problems. In other words, it's not simply the bad boys they are attracted to, but their immoral, destructive lifestyle. Bad boys also prefer women with substance problems, because they are easier to take advantage of. They are also less likely to call the police, because they would expose their own criminal activities.*

[5] (para.232) *For the women reading this book, I know there are not a lot of generous, financially stable men running around. But I'm sure you know it's better to search long and hard for a good man than to be married to a rotten one. You can help increase the number of men who know how to be a good husband by **insisting** that every male you know reads this book. And you can help your daughters by making sure every boy reads this book as soon as he learns how to read! Better yet, reading from this book (along with the Bible) to children who can't read will instill values in them that they will never forget.*

HOUR 10:

FARMER JOHN

235 It was just another day for hard-working farmer John until he received word that he had just won $50,000! He was very excited of course, and wondered what he would do with the money. He had always dreamed of owning a convertible Corvette, but he desperately needed a new tractor to plow the fields. He suddenly has a great idea and decides to buy the Corvette. He has bigger tires put on his new car and adds a hitch to the bumper so that he can attach a plow. That way he can use his new Corvette as a tractor when he needs to. The best of both worlds!

236 I shouldn't have to continue this ridiculous story, but I'm sure some men can't see the point I'm trying to make. Some will say that farmer John's idea would work and for a very short time he may be able to get some use out of his tractor/car. However, it should not take a genius to figure out what's going to happen to the car in the very near future if it's used as a tractor.

237 I would imagine that the paint job would be seriously scratched on the first day of "plowing". Furthermore, as farmer John gets in and out of the car, the interior will soon become filthy with mud and dirt. It won't be long before the windshield is smashed and the mirrors broken off. Soon the engine will get filled with all sorts of debris. It's only a matter time until the car/tractor breaks down. Farmer John will then begin to curse and blame the car (not his stupid idea) for not being as durable and tough as a tractor.

238 He will complain bitterly that the car is not reliable and durable. He reasons that a car has an engine and a steering wheel like a tractor. It has brakes and tires. It's made of metal and runs off gas just like a tractor. So why isn't it as strong and sturdy? Something must be wrong with it!

239 Farmer John just doesn't seem to grasp the difference between a tractor and a car. He doesn't understand that a tractor, unlike a car, is designed to work long and hard, it's durable and powerful. It doesn't need to be treated delicately. What it looks like is not important. An expensive car, on the other hand, needs to be treated with special care. Its looks are very important and the slightest scratch is noticed.

240 Many men, unfortunately, treat their wives like tough old tractors, riding them long and hard. It won't be long before she shows signs of wear and tear. The rough treatment will obviously damage her "exterior", but sadly, her "interior" will be damaged also. She may start to believe it is not worth the effort to be feminine, that it is no longer important to be soft and gentle. And worse yet, she may forget **how** to be soft and gentle.

241 Wouldn't it be nice if men treated their wives like an expensive car, with special care and attention? Making sure she had everything she needed, and paying constant attention to her. Noticing the smallest "scratch" and quickly coming to her aid before it got worse. And recognizing she has strengths and weaknesses, and then adjusting his treatment of her accordingly.

242 The 24:Hour Man does understand that there is a difference between men and women. He knows that women are like luxury cars and need to be treated gently. Their needs may appear exotic: special lotions, fancy perfumes, delicate clothing, etc. But the beauty that is created from this extra special treatment is beyond compare and is worth every penny!

243 When the 24:Hour Man decides to get married, it's not because he needs someone to help him pay the bills (or plow the fields). He is perfectly capable of taking care of his "farm". What he wishes to have after a long, hard day's work in the hot sun is a soft, delicate woman to soothe and refresh him like an oasis. Someone who can help him forget the troubles of the day and who can encourage him with her feminine charms to face the next. He thanks God for the blessing of a wife. And he shows his appreciation daily for the endless things she brings to his life: love, tenderness, gentleness, softness, companionship, encouragement, and children.

244 The 24:Hour Man understands that if he decides to get married it is an honor to take care of his wife. He knows that she will need certain tools to do her job of assisting him and it is his responsibility to supply those tools. He understands that in marriage, he is the marathon runner and his wife is his assistant. To continue your understanding of how the marital relationship works, let's go for a long run:

HOUR 11:
MARATHON RUNNER

245 **If** you've ever seen a marathon you know that the race begins with a group of runners packed at the starting line. (The group represents husbands in this hour.) The race begins and after a few miles an assistant standing on the sidelines will hand a runner something to drink. At other times during the race the runner will be given vital information. His assistant will provide everything he needs, including encouragement.

246 The thoughts to ponder in this hour are: Would you rather have a partner run the race with you? Or would you rather have an assistant to help you? If your assistant runs with you, you won't have anyone to aid you during the race, to supply you with water and other necessities.

247 Everyone's role in a marathon is clear; the runner runs and the assistant assists. The marriage arrangement should be just as clear; the husband goes to work to make money to take care of his family, his wife then takes care of her husband.

248 But when husband and wife both work outside the home, marriage is placed at huge disadvantage. A professional marathon runner would never consider running a race without an assistant to supply him with water, towels, and other necessities. But many men get married and find themselves running the long "marathon of marriage" unaided, because their partner is running (working) also.

249 A marathon runner needs to drink plenty of fluids during the race and it's important that he receives information about his position and pace. The person who provides these things for him is extremely important. The assistant knows the runner's needs and can usually anticipate them. The assistant can see what's ahead and relay this vital information to the runner. However, the assistant can only be useful if she has the tools to do her job.

250   If husband and wife both have jobs, not only is the husband working without an assistant (at least, not a dedicated, full-time assistant), his wife is also working without an assistant. They both have needs, but who's going to take care of them?

251   It's easy to see where this is heading. No one can take care of the needs and wants of a man better than a woman and vice versa. Friendly relationships with the opposite sex may begin innocently, but it's normal to develop feelings for a person when he or she is tending to your needs. Therefore, when one or both begin to spend time with the opposite sex, major trouble is soon on the way!

252   When wives are "forced" to work outside the home, they're not available to take care of their families, a simple fact that many people ignore or don't see as highly important. (Stay-at-home moms are now seen as a luxury, instead of a necessity, which is what they are.) When women get married, they "sign up" for the roles of wife, assistant, and mother. Their love may compel them to join in the race if needed, but I'm sure most wives would prefer to tend to their families. (Especially, if they are being fully supported.) They know that someone still has to fulfill their roles at home. So against all odds, they courageously attempt the impossible by doing two jobs at once: run the marathon (get a job) **and** assist the runners (their husbands).

253   Women know that when their husbands succeed, the family succeeds, which is why they will attempt the impossible to make it happen. The 24:Hour Man doesn't need anyone to do the impossible for him, because he does what many consider impossible; he fully supports his family! He doesn't enter into a relationship until he has achieved a level of financial stability that allows him to take care of his household.

254   The 24:Hour Man knows that when you provide a safe home for your wife, you are saying loud and clear that you love her. He knows that a wife who is truly loved will reflect love in countless ways. He will be the recipient of the special love that only women can give.

255   If you give your wife all the love you have and keep her safe from harm, what you will receive from her will be a love that is refined and enriched; love in its purest form. What you receive will be Real Love:

HOUR 12:
REAL LOVE[1]

²⁵⁶ **It** would be easy to love someone if that person were perfect, never saying or doing anything wrong. But of course, no one is perfect. Everyone has their own unique brand of imperfection. In fact, being imperfect is so easy we can do it in our sleep. All that we have to offer anyone is a flawed soul and an underdeveloped ability to love. If only we could love in a way that would "cover a multitude of sins". (1 Peter 4:8) If we could learn how to give **real** love, it would be easier for others to bear our imperfections.

²⁵⁷ We all have to work hard to overcome our sinful ways and improve our ability to love, because there is no magic love pill[2] we can take like vitamins. Fortunately, we do have an instruction manual, the Bible and an instructor, Jesus, who gave us a perfect example of what real love is. If we follow His example, we can learn how to love and make it a lot easier for others to overlook our flaws.

²⁵⁸ The way love is described in the Bible is not how it's portrayed in movies and on television with long, impassioned mountaintop speeches declaring your undying love to the world (with violins playing softly in the background). There are no flowers and no chocolates. No kisses on the beach (although the Song of Solomon is pretty spicy). The Bible's description of love (1 Corinthians 13:4-7) is much deeper. It seems that one way to look at love is:

<u>**Love is putting up with others,
even when they don't put up with you.**</u>

²⁵⁹ Not exactly what you'd expect to find in a mushy greeting card, but that is what real love is; loving others, whether they love you or not. Caring about others even though they don't care about you. Love is giving of yourself and expecting nothing in return. Can you see how this would improve **all** your relationships and especially your marriage?

260   We all know people who despite being surrounded by negativity and hate remain sweet and loving. Their love astounds us. They are proof that love conquers all and that it is indeed better to give than to receive.

261   Jesus (the ultimate 24:Hour Man!), demonstrated something else when he showed love to everyone he met, including those who hated him. He made it perfectly clear that:

Real love is consistent

262   Love is meaningless if it is not consistent. Consistency seems to be the key to everything in our lives. Consistency lets us know if love is real. This is especially important in marriage as your mate is the person you'll spend the most time with and the person who'll need your consistent love the most. To make the time spent together more enjoyable you not only have to learn what your mate likes, but you have to consistently provide those things (while also avoiding your mates dislikes). Consistent expressions of real love shows your partner that you truly care about them.

263   But as you've learned, a man who is not financially stable will have a very difficult time providing his wife anything consistently, because his attention is divided. In an effort to make money many men forget to take care of the emotional needs of their wives. Some marriages may be able to survive without financial stability for a short while, but the real danger comes when a man takes away the consistent love and affection his wife craves. She may be able to withstand many things, but lack of love and attention **is not** one of them, especially if she works outside the home!

264   Unfortunately, in many cases, not even a woman's real love can save a marriage if her husband doesn't consistently show her love and affection. When a man struggles financially he has divided loyalties, different priorities, each fighting fiercely for attention; he feels pulled in many directions. When his wife asks for the love and attention she needs and deserves, he finds it very difficult to concentrate on the task at hand. The more she asks, the more annoyed he becomes. If he's not careful he may soon be relieved of the "burden" of caring for his wife's needs when they are taken care of by someone else!

265   Most men don't understand that if they continue to give their wives the love they need, not only will it strengthen and inspire their wives to continue the battle, but they (the husband) will be refreshed as well. They don't see the connection between giving love (consistently) and receiving energy. To use a car analogy, how many car batteries have been mistakenly replaced when the alternator was the problem? Affection and attention (and also a feeling of security) is what keeps a woman's "love battery" charged. Men must understand that love is not simply something women want, it's a necessity! Just as the earth needs the sun's light and energy. The earth needs energy to create the beauty we behold all around us (and also to sustain all life). Women are also energized by love. Women use love's energy and convert it into the incomparable feminine beauty we behold everyday (and also to bear all life). (See page 145, "Beauty ain't pretty")

266   Haven't you noticed what happens when you surprise your wife with an unexpected gift? She is renewed. She blooms like the morning glory. Haven't you noticed the smile on her face when you tell her how special she is? Suddenly, she's no longer tired, her spirit is revived.

267   Whether a man is financially stable or not, he can give love, because it doesn't cost anything to show that you care. Of course, it's easier to show love if you know what love is:

Love is giving

268   Before the earth could produce the beauty we marvel at, it first had to receive the sun's light and energy. But if the sun only gave its power for one day or one week per year, the earth would not be able to produce anything. Therefore, love is not just giving, but giving freely and **consistently**. Love is giving and expecting nothing in return.

Love is knowing

269   If your wife doesn't know you love her, you're doing something wrong; it's that simple. When someone loves you, is there any doubt in your mind? When someone loves you, they show it in many ways, consistently. The 24:Hour Man never wants his wife to feel unsafe or in doubt about his love for her. When people are loved, they absolutely know you'll be there whenever they need you.

Love is understanding

270 Real love is patient, it knows that no one is perfect and actually expects imperfection and prepares for it. An understanding person accepts the good and the bad. The man of discernment knows that the vast majority of what we get from others is good. Rarely does anyone purposely do anything bad to us. And often what we consider bad is simply annoying; it's what imperfect people do. Love understands and forgives instantly.

271 Love is like the wind, you can't see it, but you can definitely see what it does and you can feel its effects. When you give love, you become that cool breeze that everybody enjoys on a spring day. Don't wait for a reason to show love, because you know everyone needs it. Try to show concern to everyone you come in contact with. Many people are dying to show love, but are not sure how it will be received. Love often opens up the floodgates to more love, so give it whether they ask for it or not, whether they deserve it or not.

> **People need love most when they deserve it least.**
> Ernest Eberhard

272 You can even show love by allowing others to express their love to you! Again Jesus demonstrates: Mary, therefore, took a pound of perfumed oil, genuine nard, very costly, and she greased the feet of Jesus and wiped his feet dry with her hair. (John 12:3)

273 Real love can often be shown by simply listening to someone's concerns. Many people just want to be heard, to feel understood. Giving a few moments of your time can make a big difference. And to consistently show that you care, can make all the difference!

274 Real love is consistently giving to others and putting up with others. Real love is making sure that the other person is happy. The 24:Hour Man is always in "giving" mode, showing interest for everyone around him and especially his wife. He is easy to identify, he is the man you see at a restaurant who always says, "Check please!":

[1] (above para.256) **Patchwork Love:** *Real Love is like a quilt, a quilt feels like love. I remember my grandmother's quilts. How heavy they were, how warm and secure they made me feel. I remember the colors and the smell. I remember the love that went into making them. Unlike the lightness of comforters, I remember the weight; how it protected me, how it soothed me. How it loved me and asked nothing in return. No matter what the day held I knew I would soon feel its comforting embrace. It was there for me every night and only wanted to hold me until I fell asleep.*

Does your love consistently make your wife feel safe? If not, buy her a quilt. Better yet, have a personalized quilt made for her and then love her like a quilt.

[2] (para.259) *What if there **was** a "Magic Love Pill"? A pill that made the taker fall completely in love with his or her mate. Would you take it or would you give it to your wife or girlfriend? Most people I've asked that question say they would give it to their mate, which shows that people like to be loved. It also shows that people are not receiving the love they need.*

Though there is no right or wrong answer to the question, I'm sure you know that a 24:Hour Man would take the pill himself. Hopefully, you've learned that to receive love, you have to give love. I believe a "Magic Love Pill" does exist, but it's not in capsule form. It's called the Bible. It, like this book, teaches the importance of giving consistently. Once you learn that lesson (swallow that pill), you will receive all the love you need.

HOUR 13:
CHECK PLEASE!

275   **When** a man and woman go out to dinner, who pays? If you've read this far and don't know the answer, you've obviously missed something. Go back to Hour: 1 and start over, because 24:Hour men know the answer to that question. Who pays for dinner is one of those questions that expose one of the main problems with our society--men not knowing what their role is or simply not accepting it. (Notice that I didn't use the word "date". It's a word you should never use, I explain why in Hour: 23, pg.140 para.459)

276   Whenever a man entertains a female (or group of females), if possible, he should always pay! There are exceptions, but never because he doesn't want to pay. Paying for meals shows that you know how to take treat a lady and that you want her to feel comfortable and secure. Not only does it make her feel special, it boosts your confidence and raises her opinion of you.

277   There are, of course, many men who think that if they always pay for dinner, some women will use them as a meal ticket. Although I have never met one, I'm sure there are some women who will take advantage of the opportunity, especially if they dine with a man who expects to be "paid back" for his "generosity." They may sense insincere motives and "reflect" insincere motives. If this situation arises remember what you learned in Hour: 2, give freely and expect nothing in return. If you truly feel you are being taken advantage of, don't associate with women you feel are not sincere, but don't let someone's lack of character change who you are.

The 24:Hour Man is generous with everyone

278   Just as the sun doesn't select a few spots on the earth to shine on, the 24:Hour Man tries to shine on every person he meets. When he dines at a restaurant, he immediately engages in conversation with the waitperson, asking his or her name, etc. This puts everyone at ease and creates a calm, pleasant atmosphere.

279   As the menu is being read, he does a quick estimate of the cost of the meal and immediately after all orders have been taken, he **pre-tips** the waiter (20 to 30 percent of the meal). He does this quietly, but if his guest notices, he simply says he's putting the waitperson at ease, because many people don't tip at all. (Many people simply don't know that the tip is the main portion of the wait-person's salary. And for those who are wondering, I am not, nor have I ever been a waiter.)

280   Pre-tipping[1] is a simple, yet powerful example of generosity and concern for others. It displays many of the qualities of the 24:Hour Man with one simple act of **pre**-kindness. This form of tipping does something else; it gives the waitperson an opportunity to show kindness in return. Tipping **after** the meal doesn't give the waiter the opportunity to show his appreciation. There's not much he or she can do as you're walking out the door.

281   Some men will say that when they go out for dinner they can't always afford to pay (and certainly can't pre-tip 20 percent) even though they would like to. To those men, I say let this be a gauge:

If you can't afford dinner, you can't afford marriage!

282   Maintaining a relationship costs a lot more than an occasional dinner at a nice restaurant. If you can't afford to take a woman out to dinner (and pre-tip properly), my advice is to let your companion find someone else to take her out, someone financially stable. If not, you may find yourself involved in a relationship before you're ready financially. You may then find yourself paying for something that's a lot more expensive than a nice dinner; a not so nice divorce!

283   Of course, I'm oversimplifying (a little), but I hope you get the point. I'll try once more to show you why it's very, very important for a man to be financially stable before he even thinks about getting into a relationship. I'm going to offer you a brand new, fully loaded Lexus:

[1] *(para.280) Pre-tipping should not be limited to restaurants. Anywhere tipping is customary, pre-tip, and observe how it brightens that person's day.*

Besides pre-tipping, I have one more thought about restaurant etiquette and the treatment of restaurant personnel in general. I have often seen people be very rude and demanding of waiters, as if abuse is a part of their jobs. To those people I would like to know how you would feel if you went to a restaurant that your daughter worked at and saw someone verbally abuse her? I'm sure you would be upset. So the next time you go out to dinner, pause before you berate your waiter, because he or she is someone's son or daughter.

HOUR 14:
LEXUS[1]

284 You receive a letter in the mail. It's from the Lexus automobile corporation. It reads: Great News! You've been chosen to participate in a special program. We would like to offer you our top of the line automobile at a once in a lifetime price, $36,000! That's half off the regular price of $72,000. And to make this offer even more incredible, your new car will be paid for in one year! That's right, only 12 easy monthly payments of $3,000. No interest! No credit check! Simply go to your nearest dealership and select your new car!

285 Many men would unwisely accept this offer relying on blind faith that they can somehow make the payments, not to mention the regular maintenance, gas, and insurance.[2] They take on this responsibility thinking they are going to give their new luxury car the best of everything: premium gas, weekly trips to the car wash to be gently hand-washed and an expensive car cover (even though it'll be parked in a spacious, climate-controlled garage!).

286 It won't be long before the $3,000 monthly payments become too much to handle. Changes have to be made. No more premium gas, regular will do. No more weekly trips to the car wash, a bucket of warm soapy water will suffice. Suddenly, your luxury car has become a luxury you can't afford. Something you "loved"[3] has now become a burden. The car has to be sold or returned to the dealership.

287 Unfortunately, men don't need a "credit check" to get married to an infinitely more "expensive" woman. Many marriages then follow a similar course as the Lexus example. A financially unstable man full of hopes and good intentions, foolishly takes on the responsibility of marriage. In the beginning, he gives his wife the best of everything, trips to the spa to be pampered from head to toe and dinners at fine restaurants.

288   But he soon realizes that marriage, although very fulfilling, can be very expensive[4] (particularly when you don't prepare for it). Changes have to be made. No more fancy restaurants, Mom's place will do. No more massages at the spa, an occasional firm hug should be sufficient. Suddenly, his beautiful wife has become a burden, a luxury he can't afford. If she isn't "sent back to the dealership", he may decide to send her to work like Farmer John. (Hour: 10, pg 65) And when he does, the marriage will begin to speed downhill faster than a Ferrari in seventh gear!

Women are like luxury cars

289   Have you noticed that the more expensive an automobile is, the more "delicate" it is and that it needs more expensive products and extra special care? Men understand this, but many don't seem to understand that women are even more delicate and need extra special care as well. Not necessarily expensive care, but definitely special, consistent care!

290   If you don't see the connection between giving your wife consistent care (maintenance) and a successful marriage, continue to read carefully. And if you are not ready, willing, and able to do what's necessary to keep a relationship running at top performance, please pay extra special attention to the rest of this book. If by the time you finish this book you don't feel it's your responsibility to fully support your wife and family, maybe you're not cut out for marriage. Maybe if you read the book again you will grasp the meaning of marriage. In the meantime, I suggest that you leave the "showroom"!

291   Many married men choose to send their wives off to work, mistakenly thinking it will help the marriage; it won't! It will only make the marriage more unstable. (As you'll see in the next hour.) A man who sends his wife away from home to work is in effect tossing a butterfly into a hornet's nest. He has opened Pandora's box[5] and now the marriage (more specifically, the wife) is completely exposed to every possible threat a marriage can face! Women, who have become accustomed to the security and protection of their home and husband, must enter the workforce to fend for themselves. Here are just 20 of the evils and miseries that will relentlessly attack your wife and your marriage:

¹(above para.284) *Ladies, please excuse the car analogies in this hour and throughout this book. These are terms men understand and can more easily relate to.*

²(para.285) *Many men go into relationships knowing they are not financially prepared. They foolishly believe that the worse that can happen is that they might break up with their wives or girlfriends. But even if you ignore the female's strong desire to bond and the incredible pain she will suffer if that bond is broken, the potential for disastrous life-altering events are plentiful: kids raised without both parents, violent episodes resulting in criminal charges on your record, physical injuries, and scars, etc. (all of which become a permanent part of the memories of everyone involved).*

³(para.286) *You may have noticed that throughout this book I've used the word "love" only when referring to people. I believe it cheapens the word "love" when it is used so freely to describe your feelings about things like chocolate or your job. This seems to be an American custom as it is not practiced in other languages. In the Spanish language, for example, "enchanted", is used instead of "love" when describing feelings associated with things other than people.*

⁴(para.288) *I reluctantly used the word "expensive" when referring to marriage. Marriage is like anything else that requires maintenance. When you purchase an automobile, you know it's going to need gas, oil, and other necessities. You prepare for accidents and every possible expense, before the purchase. You get insurance, before you need it. It works the same way with marriage. Marriage is a lot easier and a lot less "expensive" to maintain if you prepare for the expenses, before you get married!*

⁵(para.291) *To open Pandora's box means to create an **uncontrollable** situation that will cause great grief. Because women are so dedicated to their husbands and their families, they will bravely and unflinchingly face any obstacle that arises. But without a doubt, on some level, if a married woman is forced to work outside the home, she will be attacked in the workplace!*

Like lambs flung into the wilds of Africa, most married women simply aren't equipped to withstand the relentless onslaught of vicious, powerful, predatory beasts poised to consistently assault them and therefore, your marriage. Virtually every woman alive has a horror story to tell about how she narrowly managed to survive disaster. Pandora's Box may be fictional, but there is nothing make-believe about the dangers many women face when they are forced to spend long hours away from the safety of their home.

*When a man cannot afford to take care of his wife and she is forced to work outside the home, he has **absolutely no control** over what happens to her! But if something does happen to her, he must deal with the aftermath. You must now take time to try to heal and "restore" your wife. This requires a skill you may not have, which means she may need counseling, which requires even more time and more money you can't afford. It may take years before family life returns to normal. In the meantime, she has to continue to work with the person or persons who abused her!*

Illustration: You work in a large auto repair shop and others are allowed to use your tools. When you return from vacation you discover that many of your tools have been damaged. Your tools have not only been misused, but were also exposed to the weather. You must now attempt to complete your work with damaged tools. But before you can start your work, you must take time to restore them. This may require a skill you don't have, which means you will have to pay someone to repair them or replace them, which requires money you can't spare. Meanwhile, you must continue to allow others to use your tools and so the cycle continues.

I'm sure if you were faced with the illustration above your goal would be to run your own repair shop so you wouldn't be forced to work with people who abuse your tools. And I'm also sure that your wife would love to be married to a man whose goal is to make sure his wife doesn't have to associate with people who don't care for her.

HOUR 15:
20 REASONS WIVES SHOULD NOT WORK AWAY FROM HOME![1]

1 **She spends more time with other men than with her husband**

   When you spend time with someone it's normal to begin to feel comfortable with that person. Over time, it's very easy for strong feelings to develop. Need I say more?

2 **Conflict with co-workers and superiors**

   Not everyone gets along in the workplace. Your wife may face verbal abuse **daily**, simply because a co-worker is in a bad mood.

3 **Sexual harassment**

   We know that sexual harassment exists, so why put your wife in that position? If she complains, it may lead to even more abuse. (Abuse you may know nothing about, so she suffers alone.)

4 **Working with sick co-workers**

   Hopefully, the worst thing your wife catches is a cold, but obviously there are many other dangerous germs and viruses she could contract from a sick co-worker.

5 **Stress-related illnesses**

   Stress causes an endless list of physical problems. (Headaches and migraines, etc.) Mental stress alone is enough to break the spirit of many people, but the attacks on your wife won't stop because she's upset. In fact, the onslaught may get worse, because some people have no problem kicking a person when they're down.

6 Negative influence from co-workers

Your wife may be introduced to many things that harm your marriage. She'll obviously work with other women, many of whom have also been forced to work away from home; and if misery loves company, this is not the kind of company your wife should be keeping.

There will also be plenty of men for your wife to rub shoulders with (and that's not just a figure of speech). I'm pretty sure the "office hunk" will have the best interests of your marriage in mind. And don't forget the "encouragement" your wife may receive to do illegal things like stealing from work or using drugs.

7 Not readily available for emergencies

It's comforting to know that you have someone who can quickly come to your aid, someone who knows your medical history and what medicines you may need. Imagine the guilt a woman feels when she is not available to quickly come to her family's aid. (Guilt, is another reason wives should not work away from home.)

8 Less time to spend with her husband

It's difficult to bond with and stay bonded to someone you seldom see. Many women get married on Saturday and go back to work on Monday! If your wife has to work, she deserves at least one week off for a honeymoon. A good marriage is built on lots of good memories!

9 Less time to help others

Women are naturally giving and enjoy helping others, but working 8 hours a day leaves little time for them to help their community. They like the feeling of being a part of something. Women enjoy improving their environment.

10 Less time and energy to take care of herself[2]

Most working women don't have the energy, time or money to go to the gym after a long day of work. She needs just as much time to work on herself to stay beautiful and fit as she did when she met you. Ask any woman and she'll tell you, "Beauty ain't easy!", but she'll gladly do it for the man who loves and cares for her. She just needs time and of course, money.

11 Less time to take care of you[3]

Should you get sick your wife won't be available to take care of you. You'll have to wait until she gets home from work and then hope she's not too tired or stressed or sick herself, if you want the comfort only a woman can give. I'm sure your wife would love to be in a position to take care of you until you get back on your feet.

12 Women still do most of the housework

When working women get home, it's time to start their next job, housework. "A woman works from sun to sun, but a woman's work is never done". I'm sure when that quote was written it **did not** include working away from home.

13 Extra expenses

Working wives have many extra expenses. (Car payments, gas, car insurance, etc.) In fact, studies have shown that the vast majority of a working wife's earnings go to these extra expenses. Many women are almost working for nothing and I'm sure there are some cases where it **costs** money for wives to work outside the home! (Read "Two Incomes and Still Broke" by Linda Kelly)

14 Medical expenses

If your wife gets sick, she not only can't work, but you now have medical bills to pay. (Hospital charges, medicine, doctor's visits, etc.) Plus the bills she normally paid.

15 Everything she does will be rushed

When you have plenty of time to get a project done, you usually do a better job. Women who have the "luxury" of staying at home have all the time they need to take care of their home and themselves.

Working wives always feel rushed and are compelled to do many things at once. Like brushing their teeth and ironing while cooking breakfast. Often dressing and applying makeup while they drive to work. They have to be very creative with their limited time. Because women are so adaptable, they usually figure out how to squeeze 25 (or more) hours into a 24 hour day. Obviously, this pace can't be maintained forever. Stress always wins. And when she breaks down, who's going to care for the caregiver?

16 More time spent away from the safety of home

Obviously, if your wife is at or near home you don't have to worry as much about her safety. You both have peace of mind.

17 Not available to protect the home

When you have a wife to take care of your home you don't have to worry if it's properly secured. (All doors locked, windows closed, etc.)

18 No respect from in-laws and her friends

You will not receive support and respect from your in-laws if you do not take care of their daughter. And speaking from a practical standpoint, the benefits you receive from those who love your wife will often far surpass any benefit you gain from her working outside the home. If you provide your wife with a safe, loving home, you will be well-respected, not to mention admired, by everyone who knows you.

19 What affects your wife, affects you!

If you go over the list, you can easily see that whatever affects your wife will affect you. If she gets sick, you may not get sick as well, but you **will** suffer in some way.

20 The Greeting!

The reason "The Greeting!" was added to this list is because it is one of the many benefits men don't receive when their wives work away from home. The Greeting! is the sweet welcome home hugs and kisses you get from your family. It's a daily reminder that you are loved and appreciated. Men who fully take care of their wives get to come home to a happy, loving woman, a clean house, a home-cooked meal, and peace and quiet.

292 The list could be longer, but I'll stop here. Of course, if you have kids, the list does get longer: day care expenses, extra travel expenses, less time to bond with their mother, and many children won't receive the benefits of breast-feeding.

293 When a man fully supports his wife, she knows (and the world knows) that he loves her and that he values her. But the man who doesn't support his wife sends a different message. Say, for example, you were a traveling salesman who spends most of the day away from the office. Would you regularly leave your wallet, house keys, and cell phone on your desk before you left for the field? Of course not! You would never leave personal items unprotected, because you value them. Do you think your wife feels valued and loved when she's consistently left unprotected? (Many men don't feel comfortable leaving a tuna fish sandwich in the office refrigerator, but have no problem leaving their wives unprotected. This in effect means that some men value a tuna fish sandwich more than their wives!)

294 Many men send their wives, their most valuable "asset", to work alone and completely unprotected 5 or more days a week![4] Some men have never visited their wives' workplace. (This would at least let the other men know that she is married and has a husband who watches over her.) And some men don't even know the office phone number so they can call their wives. I even know of cases where women don't have a number to call their husbands if they needed them! When you send your wife off to work, miles away from the safety of her home, no matter how loudly you yell "I love you", no one will hear you, including your wife. (See Hour: 16, pg.93 para.313)

Think a new way, think old-fashioned

295 I'm not sure when or why the treatment of women changed so drastically. Or why the idea of a man fully taking care of his wife has for many men been forgotten. But we need to readjust our thinking when it

comes to caring for women. It seems they are the only ones who **everyone depends on**, but who have no one they can depend on! They are the ones who suffer the most from the modern relationship.

296   In no other area of our lives is this kind of inadequate, neglectful care accepted.[5] A man, for example, would never purposefully leave a few spark plugs out of a car's engine or continue to drive a car he knew had little or no oil. And no man would neglect to put coolant in the radiator. Yet many women go years without love's cooling effect, while their husbands ponder why their wives are always "running hot".

297   Many women, on top of not being loved and properly cared for, are expected to perform their duties, without making mistakes, without getting tired, and without complaining. They consistently perform to the best of their abilities with absolutely no signs of appreciation from their husbands. Women, it appears, are victims of their own greatness. Because of their incredible ability to adapt and eagerness to please, some men find it easy to take them for granted. Wives, who are perfectly designed to accept some of their husband's responsibilities, are often forced to assume all of them, permanently!

298   Part of the problem may be that many men have not seen the difference between male and female roles, because the line has been blurred. Women are often forced to accept any job that's available, thereby finding themselves working side-by-side with men. This further convinces many men that males and females have the exact same abilities and therefore, feel justified in treating women like men.

299   Women have gone from being helpers and assistants to substitutes and replacements for men.[6] To use a computer analogy, instead of viewing wives as external hard drives (for backup purposes **only**), many wives are being overworked, like an external drive that is required not only to store programs, music and video files, but also to run them. The problem is not that the machines can't perform these extra functions. The problems arise when the external hard drive is required to continuously and simultaneously perform several operations permanently!

300 Men have been blessed with over-qualified assistants, but women are simply not designed to perform their duties **and** their husband's duties, simultaneously, continuously, and endlessly! And to make it even more impossible for them to succeed, they must also perform **perfectly**, because they have no backup! (I don't mean to insinuate that this is a deficiency in women, because men will also crumple when over worked.) A woman's love will compel her to push her body beyond its limits. But a crash is inevitable, unless a hero "rescues" her. Hopefully, her husband will be that hero, if not see Reason 1 at the beginning of this hour.

301 I hope at this point in the book you are at least beginning to understand that there is a big difference between men and women. And I hope you see the benefits of taking care of your wife and providing her with a safe and loving home. But providing a safe home doesn't mean you've done anything extraordinary. Having a home is a part of being financially stable, which is what you should be **before** you get married. (Have I said that enough?)

302 Also, simply owning a home doesn't guarantee you will have a happy, successful marriage. As you should know by now, a lasting, happy marriage has to have two things. (There are no exceptions!) First, financial stability or more specifically, the husband must be financially stable. (Or at least, well on his way to becoming so.)

303 The next thing a good marriage needs is a confident, generous, loving husband. If you're wondering why I didn't also say a loving wife, reread Hours: 2 &12. If you want a loving wife, be a loving husband; it's that simple! If she doesn't respond to your love, wake her up, because she's probably asleep (or in love with someone else). Wives truly love (financially stable) husbands who love them, that's simple logic. Here's some more logic that will help you see marriage more clearly:

¹(above para.1) Because women naturally blend in with their environment it should be obvious that what she is exposed to in the work environment **will** have an effect on her and therefore, your marriage. Any damage that may occur in the workplace may not be easily seen, but eventually it will appear. For example, whenever someone drives your car, as soon as you sit in the driver's seat you have to readjust any settings the previous driver may have made. Now imagine someone using your car 5 days a week! Your car would constantly have to be readjusted: Seats moved back and forth, headrest raised or lowered, mirrors moved, steering wheel tilted up or down, radio stations reset, etc. And add to this, the wear and tear of different driving styles and the extra miles the car is driven. The effects of this treatment are not seen until damage has been done.

The effect is similar to the working-wife who has to behave one way at home and another at work. In many ways the workplace is worse than a controlling husband. She is told when to come and when to go, how to dress, how to speak, and when she can speak, when to go to the restroom, and for how long. She is told when and how long she can take a break. And then there is the influence she receives from male co-workers and how she has to adjust to them. She is exposed to men who in many cases don't have pure motives, yet she has to blend into the environment or appear to be a troublemaker. She then has to readjust to her husband's "driving style". As you can imagine there will occasionally be days when she has trouble at work and then come home to more trouble. Her husband who she is counting on to comfort her is obviously unaware of her circumstances at work and may inadvertently add to her mental wear and tear. Eventually this treatment will take its toll. Both the husband and wife may not see the effects of this constant adjusting and readjusting until the damage is done.

²(para.10) Women love making themselves more beautiful and if beauty is in the eye of the beholder, who gets the most benefit from all their hard work? Women naturally enjoy being beautiful, but like a rose they have thorns. They prefer to be a source of pleasantness and so are reluctant to complain, so as not to highlight her "thorns". But if she is not fully supported she will surely be exposed to unpleasant things. Many women resist the urge to express negative incidents out of fear that their beauty will lose its focus. So

they remain quiet until they can contain the pain no longer. Unfortunately, when she expresses her pain and concerns she risks being seen as a source of trouble; her "thorns" are now clearly seen.

Many problems or "thorny" issues are avoided when wives don't have to work away from home and are not exposed to men who will do whatever they can to poison her. Women in the workplace are exposed to vulgar language and constant pressure. Not to mention enticements of every kind. So if you want to see how beautiful your wife can be, give your wife a safe "garden" to grow in.

[3] *(para.11) It is extremely easy to love and care for someone who loves and cares for you. A woman's natural desire is to lovingly care for her family; obviously she has less time to do it if she has to work outside the home. The woman who doesn't have to work away from home doesn't have to spend time convincing herself that her husband loves her. In fact, her mindset is completely different from that of the working-wife.*

A woman who is allowed to stay home, wakes up each morning knowing she is the queen of her castle, not a peasant who has to help pay for a small room in the back. Just as a man is blessed if he has a loving wife, a woman knows that she is blessed to have a husband who has the ability and desire to support her fully and lovingly. It should be plain to see that the man who provides a safe and loving home for his wife will be the recipient of more love than he can handle.

[4] *(para.294) I have often told men that as far as I am concerned, sending a wife off to work is one step away from wife-abuse! My reasoning for this strong opinion is based on the fact that most men (including myself), love women who are delicate and gentle, who are sweet and as innocent as possible. We prefer women who are not muscular or overly competitive. And most men don't like women to carry weapons. The abuse (again, in my opinion) comes into play when men send these virtually defenseless women off into the workplace (and into society in general) with absolutely no protection! It is every bit as cruel as sending a lamb into a lion's den! I have no problem with a man wanting a woman who is kind and harmless as long as he knows he's 100% responsible for keeping her safe from harm.*

[5] (para.296) *To use another analogy involving cars (or anything that requires maintenance): What if you had an extra car that you weren't using and someone wanted to use it for a few months. Would you lend it out if that person told you that he didn't think it was his responsibility to maintain it? Not only would you NOT let this person borrow your car, you would think this person was insane! And yet many in society have the crazy idea that when a man marries a woman he doesn't have to care for her. If a man asked to marry your daughter and said that he doesn't think it is his responsibility to care for and protect her, **and therefore won't**, would you give him permission to marry her?*

[6] (para.299) *Women are so loving and devoted to their families that they will allow themselves to be used as substitutes for men. But as you can imagine, if you were to substitute bananas for apples in an apple pie, you will not end up with the same results, because of the intense and prolonged heat. This does not mean that there is anything wrong with bananas.*

Conversely, because a woman can't work as long and hard as a man (and retain all her feminine qualities) that doesn't mean she is inadequate in some way. It simply means she is designed to be treated differently, just as bananas and apples are prepared differently. I've never heard of an "apple split", but that doesn't mean there is anything wrong with apples.

HOUR 16:

100% LOGICAL

304 **If** you're a man, I can safely say that you're a man 100% of the time and if you have a wife, I can safely assume she's a woman, 100% of the time. Now that we've got the facts straight and you've read thus far, you should know that to have a successful marriage you must be financially stable and you must treat your wife like a woman, 100% of the time. That's not just logical, it's 100% logical!

305 Whether you are married or not, treating a woman like a woman 100% of the time is a rule that should never be broken for any reason. And just as you would never consider putting diesel fuel in a car designed for gas or replacing a tractor with a car (See Hour: 10, Farmer John), the idea of treating a woman like a man should never cross your mind. Is that 100% logical? If not, please go back to Hour: 1 and read very slowly.

306 You may be wondering if your wife or girlfriend will begin to treat you with love and kindness, if you treat her with love and kindness. In most cases the answer is, yes. But remember that the purpose of this book is to explain what it means to be a 24:Hour Man and why it's important that you give of yourself consistently. You should have learned by now that you give because that's what you were designed to do. And as you learned in Hour: 2, the 24:Hour Man expects nothing in return for what he gives.

307 But since I broached the subject, I think the odds are very high that your wife or girlfriend will indeed treat you better, if you consistently treat her with kindness.[1] (Especially, if you are financially stable and she doesn't work outside the home.) Just remember to keep her safe and treat her gently and lovingly 100% of the time. You must be consistent! You must give 100% to your relationship, because if you don't, why should she?

308 Actually, how **can** she? How can a woman give 100% to a man who treats her well during the week, but horribly on the weekends? Is she supposed to appreciate the good days and ignore the others? What if, for example, every weekend, your wife (who prepares excellent meals during the week), prepared breakfast and placed before you cold, day-old coffee, orange juice in a lipstick-stained glass, undercooked bacon, and partially burnt waffles, all served on a dirty plate? Would you show love and appreciation by eating your breakfast when she is openly treating you with contempt, when she is obviously not giving 100%? Would you thank her for the edible parts and overlook the rest? Just as eating this type of breakfast will eventually make you sick, giving less than 100% to your marriage (or any kind of relationship) will eventually make the relationship "sick".

> **A woman will not become the wife her husband wants, until her husband becomes the man she needs.**
> T24HM!*2014

³⁰⁹ If wives are indeed a reflection of their husbands, she can only give what she gets. Is it logical to think that a woman will whisper if you scream? Or cry if you're happy? And though it may seem simplistic, isn't it logical that a woman will love a man who loves her? (Assuming, of course, that he is financially stable and makes sure her basic needs are lovingly met.) A woman who is loved will reflect that love just as surely as a mirror will reflect your smile.

³¹⁰ Although it appears that women can create love out of thin air, they need at least a little love to work their magic. To be sure, women can take a grain of kindness and turn it into a mountain of love, but before she can create another mountain, you at least have to give her another grain of kindness. Those who believe you can't make a silk purse out of a sow's ear, haven't seen the handiwork of a woman in love! If you want to receive consistent love, you have to **give** consistent love.

Take care of your wife 100% of the time

³¹¹ Logically speaking, if your wife works outside the home, are you taking care of her or is she taking care of herself? You must be as logical about marriage as you are about everything else in life. If you decide to get married, a part of taking care of your wife means not requiring her to work outside the home. Taking care of her home and family is the demanding, full-time job women were specifically designed for. Most women are expert homemakers, they take pride in taking care of their family, yet most women aren't given the opportunity to do this important job.

312   The world we live in can be a dangerous place for a man, how much more so for a woman! Taking care of your wife means providing her with a comfortable home and not forcing her to fend for herself in a world where even the police aren't safe!

313   As an example of how far (literally and figuratively) a woman will go for her family, I'd like to tell you about a lady I met in Japan many years ago. I was 21, she was over 30 and had just enlisted in the US army; this alone made her unusual. And at the risk of sounding sexist, she had "housewife" written all over her and she smelled like milk and cookies.

314   What was this woman, married with children, doing in the military, thousands of miles from her family? How this small woman made it through basic training is beyond my comprehension. She didn't have an aggressive bone in her body, yet here she was sitting across from me one day as we played Scrabble.

315   We both enjoyed playing the game, but I took no delight in beating her. She always seemed distracted. After winning the first game, I decided to allow her to win the next game. I was the unofficial Scrabble champion, so I had to keep the score close so she wouldn't catch on to what I was doing. I complained bitterly the entire game about my "inability" to come up with any good words. As her victory approached, she began to smile. It was the first that time I saw joy on her face; she had defeated the champion! I have never felt so good in defeat. From that day on, she always greeted me with a smile.

316   Hollywood would complete this story by saying that I courageously protected her and that I personally escorted her back to her family in the States. But I'm no hero and this isn't Hollywood make-believe. The best that I can do is give this story a bittersweet ending, because I don't know what happened to her. There was no war at the time, so I'm sure she returned home safely. And I'm also sure that her husband (assuming she remained married) is still not taking care of her. She's probably still trying to take care of herself and her children.

³¹⁷ She's probably a grandmother now, working as a greeter at WalMart. One of the millions of married women who will work until the day they die! This is why I make it a point to try to bring a smile to the face of every woman I meet, especially working women. I don't know if I'll ever meet Pvt. Bell again, but if I do I will ask her for a rematch and I'm sure you know who's going to win.

The Million Dollar Question[2]

³¹⁸ Contrary to popular belief, providing a home for your family is only difficult because you "think" it is. We've all been told over and over that times are hard and that it takes two incomes just to survive. Times may indeed be challenging, but the facts state that approximately 30% of married women are homemakers.[3] That translates to about 30 million men who are finding ways to take care of their wives.

³¹⁹ Let's look at this from a different angle. If you ask married men, "If you were single with no children and used all your skills and abilities, what do you think your chances are of one day becoming a millionaire?" Virtually every man would say that eventually he would one day reach that goal. But ask those same men if they can support their wives and you get the "times are hard" speech. It only takes a fraction of a million dollars to support a wife, but society has convinced many men that they can't do it. Most men believe it's easier to become a millionaire than it is to support a family! Is that logical?

³²⁰ The numbers show that there are approximately 3 million millionaires and around 30 million housewives. Roughly, that means there are at least 27 million men who are not millionaires that support their wives. Clearly, you don't have to be a millionaire to take care of your wife, because **millions** of men do it. I'm not saying it's easy to support a family, but it's a lot easier if you start off on the right foot by (I think you know what's coming next) making sure you are financially stable **before** you get married. And as you read in Hour 15, do not fall into the trap of using your wife to build financial stability, because history has consistently shown that using that oft-repeated plan will assuredly weaken and eventually destroy the marriage. (Unless you have a well-thought out plan designed to quickly remove your wife from the workplace.)

⁣³²¹   What makes supporting a family much more difficult is when you do things out of order, when you start a family before you are financially stable. (Take the Alphabet Test at the end of this Hour.)[4] Look at it this way, if you had a home before you got married, would your mortgage go up after you got married? No! Would your car payment and insurance increase? No! (Actually, in some cases, your car insurance may decrease, as many insurers offer reduced rates for married men.)

³²²   The point I've repeated over and over is that marriage will be easier to manage if you prepare for it. If you are financially stable **before** marriage (I hope that phrase is echoing in your head), your marriage will have a much greater chance of success! When you do things in the correct order, you may actually **save** money when you get married! Especially when you consider you now have someone who cooks, cleans, gardens, and shops for you. (I'm sure you know this is the short list!) Not to mention you also have a personal nurse and motivational speaker.

³²³   I've heard many men say they don't like the idea of their wives, "not having anything to do", that they don't trust their wives with all that "free time".[5] If a man doesn't trust his wife, it doesn't matter if she works or not. If fact, she will have more opportunities (and more reasons) to cheat if she works. If she works, she will consistently spend lots of time with lots of men! Because women naturally reflect kindness, what do you think would happen if one of her male coworkers consistently showed her kindness (whether he has bad intentions or not)?

³²⁴   Why many men believe they should not have to fully take care of their wives (financially and emotionally) is actually 100% illogical; especially when you consider that their wives are a part of them! The fact that women so effectively blend their lives with their husbands should be looked upon as a blessing. For a man to decide he doesn't have to provide care for a woman he asked to become a part of him is totally absurd. It makes as much sense as a man walking shoeless in snow and believing not only that he doesn't have to protect his feet, but that his soon-to-be frost-bitten feet won't affect the rest of his body!

Wives vs. Lamborghinis

325   What makes the idea of a man believing that he doesn't have to take care of his wife even more foolish is that it doesn't apply in any other area of a man's life! All men know that everything in their environment needs to be taken care of; from house plants to swimming pools to pet snakes, **everything** needs to be maintained. Yet most men don't seem to know that they are required to take care of their wives also! To drive home this point, every man knows that cars need regular maintenance. And that they must see to it that the maintenance is kept up, because cars can't take care of themselves. (I'm not implying that women can't take care of themselves.)

326   It's clear that a car can't maintain itself, but what if it could? What if you could simply push a button and your car would drive itself to the gas station or tire shop? Here's where logical thinking gets tricky. Some men would determine whether or not to push the button depending on the risk of it being stolen or vandalized and how much they valued the car.

327   In other words, if they lived in a safe neighborhood and the gas station was right down the street, there wouldn't be much risk. And if the car was a seldom used, old clunker, they wouldn't care if it was stolen or vandalized. But what if you own a $200,000 Lamborghini Gallardo convertible? Would you push the button and send the car down the road with the top down, at night? Not a chance in the world, no matter what kind of neighborhood you lived in! (I think you can see where I'm going with this.)

328   Is your wife not more valuable than a car? Then why do you push that button every day, sending her out alone, (often at night, and sometimes pregnant), with absolutely no protection or alarm system! Every time you push that button you're telling your wife you don't value her, that she's just an old clunker and that you could care less if she were stolen.[6]

329   It doesn't matter if you truly love your wife or not. If you were to see a super-luxury car pass by at night, without a driver, would you assume the owner cared about it? At best, you'd think he was an idiot, because you know that sooner or later something is going to happen to that car. The same can be said about sending your "super-luxury" wife off to work. If you continually send her out alone, unprotected, and **consistently** in the company of men, sooner or later someone will attempt to "vandalize" your marriage.

How to tempt a married working woman

330 What would you do if a man your wife worked with told her he would take care of her if she were his wife? He has planted a seed in her head and he has plenty of time to make that seed grow. Each day he paints a beautiful picture of how life would be if she were with him. (He uses two techniques to win her heart, the power of anticipation and proactive kindness. I write about them in Hour: 21.)[7] Soon she will have a decision to make. She says to herself, "Should I stay in this marriage and work 24 hours a day, until the day I die or marry a (financially stable) man who says he'll treat me like a queen?" If you were a woman, what would you do?

331 Actually, if you were "lucky" and found out that someone was after your wife, the one who has a decision to make would be you. You could do nothing and hope she decides to stay with you (a dangerous choice, because she may get an even better offer), or you can do what you should have done in the first place, which is to get your finances in order so she doesn't have to work with men who tempt her. It's not her fault that men pursue her, she can't walk around with her fingers in her ears.

332 Because everyone's circumstances are different, I won't point the finger of blame at all husbands for their wives being in a dangerous position. I will simply say as I have throughout this book, that it is the husband's responsibility to keep his wife safe.

333 Some men will use "logic" and say, "If a woman leaves her husband because she has to work outside the home, she must have weak character." That's a fair statement and to those men I say that a dog rarely has one flea. By that, I mean a woman won't leave her husband for one reason. Women don't take marriage lightly. If a woman decides to leave her husband it's probably because she's not being taken care of in a number of areas. On top of not being financially supported, she's probably not having her emotional or physical needs met. In other words, her husband is flea-bitten. (I couldn't resist.)

334 If a woman works outside the home, the odds that dinner will be ready for her, that the laundry will be done, that the house will be clean, that she will have her sore feet rubbed, that the kids will be taken care of, and that she'll be greeted at the door with a hug and kiss when she gets home, are extremely slim. And yet, most women will fight to keep their one-sided marriage alive. It takes a lot for a woman to leave her husband because:

Women believe strongly in marriage

335 No woman goes into marriage thinking to herself, "I'm looking forward to cheating on my husband. I want to get a job, and work seven days a week, 12 hours a day until the day I die. And after work I want to come home and work some more. I want to work my fingers to the bone and have my family not appreciate me. I don't want to spend any time with my husband and kids. I want them to disrespect, disregard, and despise me. I'm not going to take care of myself. I'm going to gain so much weight that my husband will grow to hate the sight of me and cheat on me. I'm looking forward to getting a divorce, so I can give all my money to a lawyer. I then want to marry another jerk and waste another 10 years of my life".

> **Do not question a woman's ability to be a good wife until you can promise her love and affection, financial support and protection.**
> T24HM!*2014

336 Of course, there are many men who love their working wives. However, when a married woman is required to work outside the home, not only does she have to battle negative societal influences, but she has to accept the fact that the person who vowed to love and take care of her has broken that promise.[8] Logic says you don't grow more in love with someone you don't spend time with. So if you find yourself in a situation where your wife has to work outside the home the time you spend with her has to be extra special! (See Hours: 18 & 19)

Play the odds

337 It seems we always play the odds except when it comes to marriage! How strange it is that even in a friendly game of 21 or Blackjack,[9] no one ever asks for another card when they show 20, because the odds of getting the card you want are as bad as it can get. Yet that same person doesn't see the risks of getting married financially unstable and sending his wife off to work. He doesn't seem to understand that although the odds are stacked against his marriage, he can improve them dramatically if he fully supported his wife. She would be his ace in the hole!

³³⁸ I know that Blackjack is a game and that emotions are involved when it comes to relationships, but men are normally very logical in all areas. If you are not presently married, I am pleading with you to use logic and wait until you have established yourself financially before you even consider marriage. The odds are much more in your favor if you do.

³³⁹ If you are married now, you can greatly improve your marriage by following just two steps. Begin working on these steps immediately. You should already know what step one is:

[1] *(para.307) It's natural to want to see results for our efforts, but don't think of receiving love as the goal, think of it as a bonus. Your goal should be to make your wife feel loved. If your wife or girlfriend is very emotional it won't be long before she reflects your consistent love. If your wife happens to be the quiet, shy type it may take some time before she shows any enthusiasm. And even then it may only be in spurts. But rest assured that if you fill her heart with love she **will** reflect it. (Matthew 12:34 – For whatever is in your heart determines what you say.) For example, if she hears her friends complain that there are no good men left, the love in her heart will compel her to speak up, to defend you.*

Some men (including myself) think that if a woman doesn't openly express her feelings it may mean she's not sure about her feelings for you, as most women easily express their emotions. If you want to bring out the love that women naturally show, you may have to show love in a more open manner. Speak highly of her to others, whisper more terms of endearment in her ear, hold her more often (and read Hours: 18 & 19 carefully). In other words, set the example, give her something positive to reflect and in time she will become comfortable showing you her feelings.

[2] *(Above para.318) Variation to **The Million Dollar Question**: To show you how a simple change in thinking can make a big difference. What if you were promised a million dollars if you fully supported your wife for one year; could you do it? The only requirements would be that your wife could not have an employer and that you must maintain the same standard of living. In other words, she would not have to eat noodles every day. Very few men would turn down this offer.*

For most men it would be the easiest money they would ever make. But what they may not realize is that it would be even easier than they imagined, because they would finally see how valuable and resourceful their wives are. With a clear goal and freedom from the bonds of a typical 9 to 5 job, you would witness an explosion of energy and excitement from your wife. It goes without saying that your personal needs will be taken care of, but that's only the beginning. Notice the rules state that your wife cannot have an employer. Your wife will see immediately that the rules do not state she cannot earn money, simply that she cannot have an employer.

It is through this "loophole" that your wife will utilize her many talents. Many will sew clothing or produce baked goods to sell. Others will style hair or do taxes or babysit. The list is endless and your wife will explore everything she can do to assist you in keeping the household running smoothly. The year would go by quickly and you would see what it means to have a partner who is free to assist you. It would probably be the best year of your marriage and yet, the only thing that changed would be your thinking.

The point I'm making is that your wife will reflect your enthusiasm for your marriage. Whether your goal is to win a million dollars, get a better job or start your own business, if your wife is free to use 100% of her time and energy assisting you, that's what she'll happily do. Because every wife will take care of the man whose goal is to take care of her!

[3] (para.318) Source: US Census Bureau

[4] (para.321) To show how important doing things in order is, I'd like you to take the Alphabet Test: Along the side of a sheet of paper write the numbers 1 through 26. You begin the test by writing one letter of the alphabet by each number. You must write the letters in **completely random order** (and do not use patterns). You have a 2 minute time limit. If you take the test alone, take another sheet of paper and cover the letters as you write them (you cannot raise the sheet to look at past letters). If you have someone to write the letters for you, you cannot ask if you've already said a letter. When you finish, count your mistakes. The goal is to write each letter of the alphabet once. If you take the test with another person or persons, you can challenge each other by seeing who makes the fewest mistakes.

What I would like you to learn from the test is that you can do things a lot quicker and easier when you do them in order. (It takes about 10 seconds to recite the alphabet in order. Doing things in order is one of the points of this book.) A variation to the test is to use a partner who plays along with you by covering the letters as they write them. You should be able to see how useful a partner can be. A partner could help you make fewer mistakes in the Alphabet Test, as you could help each other remember if you've already said a letter. If you can see how helpful a partner is in a simple game, it shouldn't be difficult to understand how useful a wife can be if she's allowed to assist you with the important things in life.

⁵(para.323) *I have heard both men and women say that they don't know what they would do with "all that free time", and that they would be bored. This reminds me of something a little boy once said to me in an attempt to get me to take him to the park. Instead of saying, "I'm bored", he said, "I'm boring." If you can't find anything more worthwhile than working a typical 9 to 5, you have a "boring" imagination. There are enough exciting places to visit and things to do to fill a thousand lifetimes. Charity is a meaningful, full-time job and is always "hiring". There's always someone who needs help. But if you or your wife can't think of anything to do to occupy your "free time" just ask any child for suggestions.*

⁶(para.328) *I'm sure many men truly love their working wives, but when she's often seen alone, she draws the attention of the ever-present hordes of ravenous wolves that see her as easy prey and they will **never** stop stalking her! Many men don't understand how important (and necessary) their presence is. Even a creature as powerful as Satan, wouldn't dare approach Eve with her husband around.*

⁷(para.330) *When a man fully supports his wife there are a lot of things she is never exposed to; improper propositions in the workplace being one of them. Once the proposition is made it remains in her mind forever and as long as she's in that environment the idea has a chance to grow. It doesn't matter if she has any intention on acting on it; as long as she has to work she will think the offer is still on the table. And through no fault of her own, the more physically beautiful she is the more offers she will receive.*

⁸(para.336) ***Marriage vows*** *are promises a couple makes to each other during a wedding ceremony. These promises have traditionally included the notions of affection ("love, comfort, keep"), **faithfulness** ("forsaking all others"), **unconditionality** ("for richer or for poorer", "in sickness and in health"), and **permanence** ("as long as we both shall live", "until death do us part").*
Source: Wikipedia

⁹(para.337) *24:Hour Men are not gamblers. I used Blackjack only as an example.*

HOUR 17:

STEP ONE: FINANCIAL STABILITY

340 **The** first step to improve your marriage should not be a mystery if you've read up till now. The best way to increase the quality of your marriage is to get your finances under control and fully support your wife.[1] I believe it's the **only** way to give your relationship the stability it needs.

341 Notice that step one has two parts. First, you must achieve a level of financial stability and second, you must fully support your wife. If you aren't willing and able to accomplish this, your relationship will always be rocky.

342 If you are married, becoming financially stable should be one of your top priorities. Draw up a plan that you and your wife agree on and then work your plan. You can both look for opportunities for you to earn more money. You must set a financial goal and once that goal is achieved, immediately remove your wife from the workforce. If it's possible to find your wife an easy, stress-free, at-home job until you're able to fully take care of her, that's better than her working outside the home. Again, I must stress that it is very important that your wife feel both safe and loved.

343 The plan you create has to be agreed on by both of you. She may feel uncomfortable adjusting to the idea of fully depending on you after years of depending on herself. You must do whatever you can to make her feel secure. Open a bank account for her. Get life insurance. Until she feels safe, she may be resistant to the changes, but your consistent hard work will eventually convince her that your actions will improve the marriage.

344 Trying to balance work and marriage can be very difficult, but don't forget that your wife needs attention also. Obviously, you can't spend long hours at work and spend lots of time with your wife. This is why I've stressed the importance of being financially stable before marriage. To help keep your marriage strong while you build a solid financial foundation, you need to know the special second step to keep your wife happy and reassured. It's called PYW, F!:

[1] (para.340) *Marriage requires constant adjusting, especially at the beginning. If you start a marriage on solid financial ground, those adjustments will go smoother. Like a roller coaster, marriage is most thrilling **after** you've reached the top (after you're financially stable), then you can let the momentum take you the rest of the way. That is to say, you can focus on pleasing each other and enjoying life as opposed to focusing on paying bills.*

Instead of enjoying marriage, couples in financially unstable marriages spend a lot of time trying to justify it. The decision to get married is questioned every day when you struggle with one lack-of-money created problem after another. Wives who also have to work outside the home need lots of assurance and constant reassurance. Why? Because the most fundamental principle of marriage, a husband supporting his wife has been broken. She needs reassurance almost daily, because she's reminded almost daily that she is not being supported and is surely not being cherished. When a working woman sees another woman being spoiled by her husband she feels devastated. She has to once again convince herself that she made the right choice.

Fortunately for married men, their working wives don't spend a lot of time with women who don't work outside the home, because their wives are at work! But imagine their frustration and heartbreak if they did. They would see others living the life they wanted and they would have to accept the fact that they may never have it. If your wife works outside the home pay special attention to Hours: 18 & 19.

HOUR 18:
STEP TWO: PYW, F!

³⁴⁵ **Whether** you are financially stable or not, you should begin step two immediately. If you want to quickly improve and strengthen your marriage, **pamper your wife, frequently!** Commit those four words to memory.

Pampering means paying constant attention to and taking care of your wife's needs and desires.

³⁴⁶ Pampering means doing extra special things only for your wife! The goal of pampering is to make your wife smile. Pampering lets her know you love her, that you're thinking about her and that she's important. Her smile will be a gauge, the more she smiles the happier your marriage will be.

³⁴⁷ Although pampering is a fun game, it is a very important and powerful tool; other than being fully supported, nothing makes a woman feel more special. Use this tool to arouse feelings in her that every woman wants: to be adored, to be wanted, to be appreciated.

³⁴⁸ Massages, poetry, love notes, breakfast in bed, flowers, and gifts for no particular reason (done regularly) are all a part of pampering. Pampering entails many different actions, but they all send the same message: I love you, I want you to be happy, I'm glad you're my wife.

> **We may not have it all together, but together we have it all.**
> Author unknown

³⁴⁹ One of the keys to pampering is consistency. (There's that word again.) Constant loving-attention tells her that insuring her happiness is your most important job. It tells her that you want her to stay forever. Don't worry about "spoiling" your wife, you can't "over-love" her, although by pampering her, she may try to over-love you! But tell her to relax, because she can't give you all her love in one day, you have a lifetime to be together. She will give you all the love you can handle, especially if you know **how** to pamper her:

HOUR 19:
HOW TO PAMPER YOUR WIFE

350 **Before** you begin to pamper your wife, there's something you must do first. It's important that you apologize to her for not being the husband she dreamed of. Apologizing acknowledges that you know there's been a problem and that you will take full responsibility to make things better. It also tells her that the changes you are making are for the betterment of your marriage and that she doesn't have to be suspicious of the "new" you. If you're not comfortable stating these words, buy a card and write your apology along with your plans for the family.[1]

351 While I can't tell you exactly how to pamper your wife, (only you know what she likes), what I can tell you is how to make your pampering a little better. Try to "personalize" anything you give or do for her. If she likes roses and her favorite color is pink, buy her pink roses. If she likes chocolate and she was born in France, buy her chocolates imported from France. Make her gifts as personal as possible. It only takes a little thought and eventually it will become second nature.

The importance of personalization

352 I'd like to share a personal experience from my childhood about gift-giving. When I was about twelve years old, my three younger brothers and I decided to buy our mother a gift. It was a perfume set. We spent all the money we had (around $15). We were very excited when we handed her the wrapped present and even more so when we saw the surprised look on her face.

353 I've always been attuned to the feelings of others, so I was confused when I noticed that her expression changed after she unwrapped the gift. She had a slight look of disappointment on her face that she tried to cover with a false smile. (My brothers didn't notice.) She thanked and kissed us, but something wasn't right.

³⁵⁴ I sat and thought for a few moments and then it dawned on me what that look meant. My mother was an Avon representative and the last thing she wanted or needed was more perfume. She was probably thinking she had the dumbest kids on the face of the earth and since I was the oldest, that meant that I was the dumbest kid on the face of the earth! Needless to say, I learned a valuable lesson and since that moment I have always tried to put thought into every gift I gave.

It truly is the thought that counts

³⁵⁵ The cost of a gift does not matter as much as the thought behind it and nothing shows as much forethought as personalization. Well thought-out, personalized gifts have special meaning. If my brothers and I had given our mother perfume that happened to have her name on the bottle or the name of her hometown that would have made the gift unique. If she was a collector of dolphin figurines and the bottle was shaped like a dolphin that would have shown that thought went into to our decision. It *is* the thought that counts, but keep in mind, the more inexpensive the gift, the more you should think!

³⁵⁶ Many men don't understand that gifts require forethought. Very often men give their wives the first thing they see. If no thought(fulness) is involved, no sincere appreciation will be shown. Men are then left scratching their heads, wondering what they did wrong.

³⁵⁷ Expensive gifts don't require a lot of forethought. For example, if you buy your wife a $500 gold necklace, the only thing you have to think about is whether she prefers regular gold or white gold. A new car, two or four doors? A trip to the spa, Saturday or Sunday?

³⁵⁸ Inexpensive gifts require lots of forethought. There has to be a clear, obvious reason for it. A $10 bracelet that resembles the one she lost when she was a child would be a great gift. Or, if you take one photograph of yourself and one of her, and combine them signifying how you've blended your lives together, that would be a beautiful, carefully thought out gift. A simple gift can become a great gift if you give it some forethought.

Sugar Pie, Honey Bunch

³⁵⁹ Another way to make your wife or girlfriend feel special is to give her lots of sweet, cute, funny nicknames. Nicknames that only the two of you know the true meaning of. Whenever she hears those words, they will remind her of you. **(WARNING: Never** call anyone else those nicknames!**)**

> **There's only one you, that's great because you're the only one I want!**
> T24HM!*2014

³⁶⁰ You've probably noticed that I've said nothing about your wife pampering you. Don't forget the point of this book, improving how men relate to others. And remember that wives are a reflection of their husbands. A happy wife will automatically pamper her husband. Women are masters at pampering, yours will pale in comparison! Also, remember that you don't give because you want something in return. You probably won't experience your wife's skill at pampering until she's taken out of the workforce, so don't be disappointed if she doesn't immediately respond in kind. Rest assured that she will, in time, give you all the love and affection you've ever wanted!

³⁶¹ Now that you know the first two steps to a successful marriage, I'd like to show you an example of one. Hollywood rarely shows a successful marriage in its movies and television doesn't do much better, but there is one man who takes excellent care of his wife, (even though he's **not** a 24:Hour Man!), Dr. Phil:

[1](para.350) *To show your wife how serious you are about insuring her happiness, buy her one of those romantic love cards that has one side blank and on that side write the numbers 1 through 30. Every night for thirty days ask your wife to write what she wants you to do for her the following day. For example, rub her feet, wash her car or do the laundry. Have her do this every night before she goes to bed, this will allow you time to mentally prepare how to make it a part of the following day. Tell her to choose something different every day if possible, but if she wants you to wash the dishes every day, that's what you do. (As an extra bonus, tell her to write two assignments on Friday nights, if you don't have to work on Saturday.)*

As you can imagine, showing her honor, love, and attention in this way will not only make her feel special and pampered, but it will also help you refocus on loving her. It will help convince her that she is your number one priority. It will be a month both of you will never forget. At the end of the 30 days both of you sign the card; she is now a CPW (Certified Pampered Woman). As regular "marriage maintenance", once a year you should give her a card and pamper her for a week; remember, a good marriage is built on lots of good memories!

*For the few men who are having trouble with the 24:Hour Man concept, the answer is "No", you **do not** ask her to do the same for you!*

HOUR 20:

DR. PHIL: A 23:HOUR MAN

362 **Dr. Phil**[1] is one of the few public examples we have of a man who knows how to take care of a wife.[2] We have very few positive male role models in our society and the negative consequences of this void are seen daily. His example shines brightly in our misguided and unguided culture.

363 Dr. Phil is a near-perfect example of how a husband should treat his wife. In fact, if every man treated his wife like he treats his, he wouldn't have a show. Watching him from a distance I can see that he cares for her and wants to keep her happy and safe. And as I've stated over and over in this book, financial stability is what gives him the ability to fulfill his role as a husband, along with the desire to be a good husband. Although, (according to Dr. Phil) he did not wait until he was financially secure before getting married, taking care of his wife and family has always been his top priority.

364 The point of this hour, however, is not simply to sing Dr. Phil's praises, as I'm sure you're wondering why I did not refer to him as a 24:Hour Man. The omission has little to do with his treatment of his wife, which is exemplary. I withhold the designation for three reasons. The first is because of his use of profanity in the presence of women (albeit in the context of his show). I believe a man should never use foul language in mixed company, especially when there are alternatives to get the point across.

365 Second, it appears he "suffers" (as many men do, although to a lesser degree) from the idea that men and women are the same and should be treated as such (excluding his wife, of course). I've seen him put intense heat on women in bad relationships, who in many cases are forced to endure harsh treatment from their husbands or boyfriends. He often questions women as if they are to blame for the way they are being treated. I say forced, because most women quickly entrench their lives into their relationships. They innately understand that they must quickly blend their lives with their husbands, to become as one, as soon as possible, so that doubt doesn't have a chance to grow.

³⁶⁶ Once roots are established it's not easy to leave, no matter how bad the relationship is. Which is why I believe it is not the wife's fault if her husband is abusive to her and she doesn't leave at the first sign of trouble. Yet, Dr. Phil will raise his voice at abused women in an accusatory manner, as though they are to blame for being abused! I can only imagine how confused the women must feel, not to mention the millions of women who watch the show.

³⁶⁷ Women in abusive relationships are not ignorant, as many believe them to be. They are faced with a dilemma that forces them to juggle several difficult options.³ At a certain point, most women do face the fact that they must leave or risk serious injury. But leaving a bad relationship **does not** mean a woman is now safe, especially if she has children. (Over 70% of domestic violence murders happen **after** the victim has ended the relationship!) I have seen Dr. Phil bring many women to tears before he attempts to offer his advice. He doesn't seem to realize that no matter what kind of advice he gives the women on his show, the "help" he gives will be temporary at best, because women are not responsible for how their mates treat them. He is in effect blaming women for bruising their husband's knuckles by repeatedly hitting their husband's fists with their faces!

³⁶⁸ Dr. Phil's treatment of the women on his program is even more peculiar when you notice how he defends his staff. He makes it clear that he is responsible for everything that pertains to his show and he will not allow anyone to attack the integrity of his team. But he doesn't encourage the men on his program to have that same sense of leadership. He understands that his staff has limited authority and like a good leader, accepts the responsibility of protecting his crew. He also makes sure they have everything they need to complete their jobs.

³⁶⁹ But for reasons unknown, he doesn't seem to understand that many women have limited authority in their marriage, but are held completely responsible for the failings of their husbands. His treatment of abused women is comparable to blaming the **co-pilot** for every delayed departure and every rough landing. Add to that, the fact that most women are not provided with the materials they need to take care of their families, but are expected to fulfill their roles (and in many cases, their husband's roles) perfectly! Sadly, they must accomplish this without protection. In fact, many need protection from the very person who promised to keep them safe!

370 Women are often forced to take the lead in their relationships and are then criticized for not being submissive! Oddly, when a woman assumes the male role that was foisted upon her, she is called a control freak or the b-word or worse. On the other hand, if she dutifully follows the lead of her incompetent and/or violent (financially unstable) husband and finds herself part of a bad marriage, she is criticized for not doing something! No matter what she does she's criticized as if she were the head of the household.

371 Many women choose to stick it out as long as they can in the hope that things will get better. They reason that as long as one partner in the marriage is willing to try, they have at least a 50-50 chance of working things out. So they choose to stay and fight (literally and figuratively).

372 Abused women are told repeatedly by everyone (including Dr. Phil) to leave bad relationships. It's easy to tell someone to leave, but the hard part is how and when.[4] I would like to ask Dr. Phil, when is the best time for a woman to leave a bad relationship? Should she keep a marital scorecard? Should she leave after two affairs, six verbal assaults and three beatings? Or, is it four affairs, fifteen verbal assaults, and two beatings? (And that's just scratching the surface when it comes to the abuses many women suffer.)

Nowhere to turn

373 Women are encouraged to submit to their husbands, whether he treats her well or not. But if his treatment of her is abusive, she is presented with several no-win choices. Many people say a woman should leave after the first attack. So let's play this scenario out. If she manages to escape without being hospitalized, she can call the police and if he is arrested, she has at best a few days to pack up and leave. In most cases, she can't go to her parents or friends (who would then become vulnerable to his wrath) or anywhere she knows he may look, which includes her job, which means she will lose her source of income.

374 Many women turn to shelters. I don't know how shelters operate, but I doubt you are allowed to stay forever. At some point she has to leave and when she does she has to hit the ground running. She will have to constantly look over her shoulder as if she were a fugitive, possibly for the rest of her

life. She has to live her life as if she were in the witness protection program, only without the protection! She may have to abandon all her loved ones or place them at risk as well. And this scenario does not take into account children.

375 Women who leave may soon find themselves homeless and penniless. They are punished for the crime of loving their husbands. And in many cases they won't be able to rest until their abuser is dead. In fact, as strange as it sounds, a woman may be better off committing a crime and being sent to the "safety" of prison! At least she'll have a "safe" place to live and receive tasty meals. Prison (and shelters) seems to be the only place a woman can go to protect herself. And oddly, she will probably receive more compassion from the inmates (many of whom have similar experiences) than from society in general! How's that for the ultimate in no-win choices!

376 As you can see, women often find themselves in horrible situations with nowhere to turn. Many women may believe they are showing concern for society by staying in abusive relationships. They know that if they leave everyone they know is at risk and if she goes to a shelter, she believes she is a financial burden to her community. It just seems "easier" to suffer quietly and maybe her martyrdom will be a lesson for others. But, unless that lesson is, "don't get involved with a man who can't or won't love and fully support you", I'm not sure what is gained by her sacrifice. And once she's paid the ultimate price, who is going to tell her story?

Even educated men don't get it!

377 Dr. Phil, like most men, doesn't seem to realize how intimidating we (men) can be to women. Even educated men sometimes treat women like men. Using harsh, vulgar language in their presence or expecting them to carry the same physical workload (often while pregnant). And then there's the ultimate in treating women like men, physical abuse. I have seen many abused women, but I have never seen a man abused by a woman, at least not to the same extreme level. (There are no battered men's shelters.) If leaving were as simple as many people believe it is, lots of women would do it and then face abuse from society for not sticking it out!

³⁷⁸ The third reason that I do not consider Dr. Phil a 24:Hour Man is that he, in an effort to be entertaining and "open-minded", relaxes his beliefs and unwittingly introduces evil to malleable minds. For example, he has allowed so-called psychics to appear on his program. By having these scammers appear on his show, he gives them credibility and furthers the belief that many people have; that these so-called psychics can actually "talk to the dead". (This oxymoronic phrase is a **ridiculous, illogical lie** that is stated so often that many now have accepted it as a fact. It is a play on words as we can all "talk" to the dead, but the dead can't talk back. See page 165.)

³⁷⁹ I say he "relaxes" his beliefs, because he acknowledges that he does not believe in these so-called psychics. I'm sure he would never allow someone he believed to be a phony to come to his home and give a "reading", but he allows them to enter the homes of his audience! These so-called psychics are even allowed to promote their books, in other words, they are allowed to do everything but sacrifice a chicken on stage.

³⁸⁰ **RANT ALERT:** Although I admire the way Dr. Phil takes care of his family and truly appreciate his desire to help others, that's as far as the admiration goes. I believe he's been knocked silly by the "conformity stick". (The pressure society uses to force everyone to go with the flow.) The world and especially Hollywood, tosses every conceivable sin into a blender and mixes it until evil looks appetizing. It's loaded with artificial sweeteners, radioactive MSG and salted with the Devil's sweat; and though you'll find this terrible tea in the non-alcoholic section, it is most certainly "666 proof". The highly concentrated mixture is sold in bottles labeled "Peace and Harmony" and marketed as "Love" juice. But don't let the smooth taste fool ya and don't hasten to swallow the worm(wood) at the bottom of the bottle, because this wicked ipecac won't taste as sweet coming back up! Dr. Phil in an apparent stupor is one of the pitchman for this unholy concoction. He assists in selling Satan's cocktail, but not before adding his own flavor packet by furthering the promotion of spiritism, gambling, and alternative lifestyles. By doing so, I find it hard to swallow anything he says.

Marriage counseling doesn't work!

³⁸¹ According to Dr. Phil himself, two-thirds of couples, married or otherwise, who attend relationship counseling, are worse or at least no better after one year. Dr. Phil has admitted in one of his books that **marriage**

counseling does not work, yet he continues to offer counseling! He doesn't seem to notice that virtually every couple that appears on his show has the same problem, financial instability; or more specifically, a financially unstable man.[5] He doesn't seem to understand that financial instability causes many husbands to have a lack of confidence, because they cannot properly provide for their families. This in turn causes their wives to feel unsafe and insecure, ergo, severe relationship problems.

[382] Dr. Phil attempts to work his magic with these couples, but as long as money problems exist, major relationship problems will exist![6] The most that can be accomplished through counseling is that the couple will agree to treat each other better. But it won't be long before the next money issue arises, and breaks that agreement.

[383] A good counselor may teach couples how to treat each other with kindness and understanding, but until a man feels in control of his surroundings, he won't feel confident. No matter what he does, that feeling of confidence will rise and fall like the temperature. A better-paying job can cure what ails many marriages, not paying someone to tell you that you should love each other.

[384] Of course, making more money and feeling more confident is only half the solution to strengthening a relationship; couples will always have to make adjustments. But two secure people who truly love each other will always **want** to make those adjustments. (Especially, if the financially stable husband is setting a proper, loving example by fully supporting his wife.)

The first 24:Hour Man

[385] My grandfather was probably the first 24:Hour Man I ever met. He and his wife owned a house and some land in east Texas. They also had a variety of animals. I vividly remember a visit to my grandparent's home one hot summer day. My brothers and I were doing what boys normally do, climbing trees and throwing anything we could pick up. We also enjoyed one of our favorite sports, chasing cows.

⁣386   The reason this particular day stands out in my mind is because it is one of the first memories I have of my grandfather walking among his cows. I was absolutely fascinated by the sight of him touching them and how they accepted him into their herd. They were so relaxed that most of the cows paid no attention to him.

⁣387   When I was a child I wanted to know how he was able to walk among his animals. As an adult I realize that it wasn't magic or some special cow-whispering ability my grandfather had, he was simply being himself. He was exhibiting the "magic" qualities of a 24:Hour Man. Qualities that even animals understand.

⁣388   My grandfather's consistent gentleness convinced all his animals that he was kind and harmless. Because of the gentle way he treated them, they didn't "think" he was harmless, they "knew" it. (Love is knowing.)

⁣389   He had to learn how to behave around them. He spoke softly and walked gracefully. He learned where and how to touch them so as not to startle them. The cows couldn't tell him how they liked to be treated, he had to put forth the effort to learn their ways and adjust to them. (Love is understanding.)

⁣390   He provided them everything they needed, when they needed it. He gave them more than just food and water (not to mention protection from predators and rock-throwing kids), he gave them himself, although they didn't (and obviously couldn't) give him anything in return. (Love is giving without expecting anything in return.)

⁣391   Of course, the secret to making this kind of relationship work is the same for all relationships, consistency. Or more specifically, consistently giving a person (or animal) what they need. Notice also that my grandfather had to be the one to take the initiative. He set the tone for the relationship. He had to determine how to act in their company and he had to learn what to feed them and how to protect them. Simply showing them that he wasn't a threat was the least of his concerns; his intent was to make it clear that whenever he was around, his animals would feel safe. His presence always meant something good was about to happen.

⁣^392^ As you can see a good leader sets the example. A gentle leader who gives consistently and expects nothing in return, is easy for anyone or any animal to follow. Of course, you may be thinking that animals can't give anything in return. But is that really the case? Are animals incapable of showing appreciation?

^393^ At the risk of sounding contradictory, when we give, we do receive something for our efforts. I know I've said to give without expecting anything in return, but the two, giving and receiving, are so intertwined that it's difficult to separate them.[7]

^394^ When we give, we always receive something in return, feedback. (Whether we perceive the feedback as negative or positive we can learn from it.) The reason I've stressed giving and not expecting anything in return is because as imperfect humans we have a tendency to use that feedback to determine whether or not to continue giving. (How many times have you heard someone who's been disappointed say, "I'm never going to help anyone ever again!"?)

^395^ For example, what if you bought a friend a gift (personalized, of course) and he didn't appear to like it or showed no apparent appreciation for it. The normal tendency to this "negative" feedback is to avoid doing anything for this person in the future.[8] There may be a dozen sound reasons for the "negative" feedback (illness, stress, medication, etc.), none of which having anything to do with you or your gift.

^396^ What if you decided to avoid a person because they didn't show the "proper appreciation" for a gift you gave them and then sometime later you discovered that he was suffering from a serious illness? (Thus explaining his lack of enthusiasm.) You would feel bad, of course, because now you understand his reaction.

^397^ And even though we receive a feeling of satisfaction from "positive" feedback, it shouldn't be used as a gauge to determine who we give to. The only reason to pay attention to positive or negative feedback is to improve how we give. Had I allowed my mother's "negative" feedback to upset me I would have never learned the secret to gift giving. (See Hour: 19, pg.106 para.352-354) Did my grandfather receive feedback from the cows? Of course, he did.

³⁹⁸ The cows showed their appreciation (positive feedback) in a variety of ways, from gently rubbing against him, to closing their eyes when he touched them. But like I said, my grandfather was a 24:Hour Man, he would have continued to care for his animals even if the feedback was "negative". He gave because that's the kind of person he was, not to get anything in return.[9] My grandfather was a 24:Hour Man, he never changed. He gave to everyone and every animal, no matter the feedback.

³⁹⁹ Of course, dealing with people is not the same as dealing with animals. I'm not an animal behaviorist, but it seems as though animals don't have a lot of moods. Dogs almost always seem happy, unlike people. To deal with the wide range of human emotions, here are 4 simple, but powerful techniques to help you adjust to others and especially your mate:

[1](para.362) *Dr. Phil is a television personality, author, and former psychologist.*

[2](para.362) *Along with Dr. Phil, there are also 30 million men who are fully supporting their wives. Most of these men are not public figures, but they deserve praise as well.*

[3](para.367) *Even good relationships have ups and downs, but the low points in bad, abusive relationships are far worse, which leads to the following dilemma: when a woman's abusive husband calms down after a violent encounter and asks for forgiveness, his passionate affection is intoxicating. The woman is at once confused and euphoric, because of the loving attention and promises. "Surely there must be some good in a man who can be this passionate and loving," she says to herself. She reasons that the Bible says we are to forgive and when he's not upset he's very loving. She recalls that she's made a commitment to stay with him. She obviously doesn't know if he will permanently change his ways, so should she stay or leave and lose all she's invested in the relationship? She's not sure if she's breaking God's law if she leaves, so most women stay, hoping for the best.*

When we marry we understand it's for better or worse, but is there no limit to the "worse"? I don't know where the line is and trying to find it is not the point of this book. I choose instead to encourage men to strive for financial stability. And once that goal is attained, to use their resources to help as many people as possible, starting with their families.

[4](para.372) *I am not suggesting that a woman should stay in an abusive relationship. The point I am trying to make is that **husbands** should receive the advice on how to improve the marriage. They should be the focus of the discussion, because they are the leaders of the family.*

Notice that I did not say husbands should be scolded or berated for their actions, as this will not produce positive results. Just as belittling and calling an uneducated person an idiot won't turn him into a genius. In fact, reprimanding an abusive husband may make the situation worse. Most bad husbands are bad simply because they don't know how to be good husbands and most of them are also financially unstable.

As stated in the foreword, what men need are positive role models and an understanding that they are responsible for their families, if they have one. The point of this book is to teach the leader how to lead.

[5] *(para.381) Many couples struggle even though they seem to be financially stable, but if the wife is working outside the home their stability is shaky at best. (Recall Hour: 2, pg.23 para.87-89 and Hour: 15) A financially stable marriage is led by a man who is financially stable; a man who is able to **fully** support his family and who **never** expects his wife to work outside the home.*

Note that women who don't work outside the home, but have husbands that pressure them to, don't feel any more secure in their marriage than women who actually work outside the home! They are often treated as if they bring nothing to the marriage unless they bring home money, overlooking everything else they do.

[6] *(para.382) Instead of counseling, Dr. Phil could help every couple that appears on his show by loaning the husband $20,000 and instructing him to take care of his bills and take care of his wife. But of course, the problems will return soon after the money runs out in most cases. This is why I've stated that when it comes to maintaining a healthy marriage, you must have a consistent positive cash flow and you must take care of your wife and family.*

[7] *(para.393) An example of how giving and receiving are intertwined would be a sensual massage. When you give your wife a massage you receive almost as much pleasure as she does as you explore the unique female body. Notice how soft and smooth her skin is. How she moans her appreciation. I'm not sure who receives the most pleasure from a sensual massage, but I'm sure your wife will get the hot oil ready whenever you want to try to figure it out.*

[8] *(para.395) Many years ago I worked as a cashier at a convenience store. A few mornings a week an elderly man would come in and buy coffee. I would thank him for every purchase and yet he would neither acknowledge what I said nor make eye contact with me. I could have easily let this "negative" treatment be an excuse to treat him negatively, but I didn't. I learned at a young age not to let someone else change who you are.*

After several months of this routine he once again entered the store and I prepared myself to be ignored. After he purchased his morning coffee I once again thanked him with as much enthusiasm as the first time I met him. But for the first and only time (I never saw him again), without making eye contact, he responded, "Thank you".

I don't know why he chose to speak to me on this fine day or why he hadn't previously acknowledged me. Maybe I was a replacement for his favorite cashier or maybe he couldn't talk before he had his morning coffee. Whatever the reason, had I stopped thanking him he would have never said a word to me. And I would not have mentioned him in this book. So what's the point of this little story? Mainly, that a 24:Hour Man never changes. He treats everyone with respect no matter how he's treated. So once again to all my former customers (and one customer in particular), "Thank you!"

[9] *(para.398) My grandfather sold many of his animals, so he did receive something for his efforts. But his care for his animals went far beyond treating them as future profit. He truly cared for them.*

HOUR 21:
4 POWERFUL RELATIONSHIP STRENGTHENING TECHNIQUES

1. The Theory of Intent

⁴⁰⁰ **If** you ever feel wronged by someone, keep one thought in mind. What was his or her intent? Did he or she intend to hurt me or was it an accident? If it was an accident, you should develop the ability to quickly forgive. You know that mistakes are a part of life and that you have made many mistakes yourself. Making mistakes is what imperfect people do. When a person makes an error, he or she is probably upset, especially if it's a major mistake, but a person who has a forgiving nature, calms and comforts.

⁴⁰¹ When it comes to being understanding and forgiving, women are behind only God and his son. The things women forgive and overlook are legendary. Your wife should be the easiest person on earth to forgive, because she has probably forgiven you dozens of times and will continue to do so. You can make it easier for her to forgive you in the future by quickly forgiving her when she makes a mistake.

⁴⁰² The Theory of Intent has a second proactive part. There's a philosophy in business that says if your business is losing money, you don't cut back on expenses in an effort to save money. Instead, you spend money on things that are designed to make more money. In the short term, this may be a strain, but if you're in business for the long term, this is a wise course of action.

⁴⁰³ In marriage or any other close relationship, you can use this same technique. For example, if you have a teenager who occasionally goes over his or her cell phone minutes, bring to mind the Theory of Intent. Did he purposely go over his minutes in an effort to hurt me? In most cases the answer is no. Was he careless? Probably, but even adults go over their minutes; it happens every day.

⁴⁰⁴ It should only take a few seconds to calm down after you see the bill. Now it's time to be proactive. Instead of taking your teen's phone, increase the allowed minutes (or find a more suitable plan). This may be a strain in the short term, but you're in the "parenting business" for the long term. Your understanding example shows your teen how to handle things calmly, lovingly, and intelligently. Isn't that how you want your teen to handle problems when he or she grows up?

⁴⁰⁵ Using this proactive technique shows your wife that you are an understanding mate that she can come to when she makes a mistake. It's love in action. It shows her that you will love and forgive her, come what may. The proactive person looks for solutions and usually finds one.

⁴⁰⁶ In time, your calm, understanding nature will keep you peaceful even when people intentionally wrong you.[1] A person who hurts you intentionally needs forgiveness also.

2. The Power of Anticipation

⁴⁰⁷ Want an example of The Power of Anticipation? How did you feel when you read the cover of this book and when you went through the table of contents? Did you feel hopeful that you might learn something that could help your relationship(s)?

⁴⁰⁸ Use the power of anticipation by scattering unusual, exciting events in the future. For example, tell your wife you have planned something special for your upcoming anniversary, like a cruise to the Bahamas![2] Tell her you heard about a new restaurant that serves her favorite foods and that you will take her there this weekend. Or mention that a new state-of-the-art cell phone will be available soon and you're going to get one for each of you. Every woman has a God-given right to be kissed under a waterfall or on a moonlit beach; tell the woman in your life those are some of the many goals you have for her.

⁴⁰⁹ The possibilities are endless. If you and your wife are **continually looking forward to exciting events**, it will add excitement to your marriage. I don't think I need to tell you what kind of love an excited woman is capable of!

3. Proactive Kindness

⁴¹⁰ You've already been introduced to the power of proactive kindness (Hour: 2, pg.25 para.96) and how it can brighten a person's day.[3] It works the same with your personal relationships and in particular, your marriage.

⁴¹¹ Proactive kindness simply means doing something for someone without being asked or waiting to be shown kindness before you respond in kind. It's kindness in advance. Why wait for your wife to ask for a foot massage? Get the hot oil ready! You know she likes romantic movies, buy her a movie pass and put it in her purse. When you look at a full moon, why does she have to ask for a kiss? Pucker up, man! Are you still reading? What'cha waiting for?

4. Let's Make A Deal![4]

⁴¹² The majority of issues that come up in a relationship can be handled in a playful, loving way. Even when dealing with those annoying habits we all have. If your spouse has a habit that you just can't accept, make her a deal. Tell her if she'll stop doing something that annoys you, you'll stop doing something that annoys her. The penalty for breaking the deal? Breakfast in bed! (These are permanent deals. If someone slips up, the penalty is paid and the deal continues.)

⁴¹³ All these techniques require the same thing, consistent effort. If difficulties arise, you now have the tools to fix almost any problem. Use these techniques throughout your marriage to keep your relationship on track and running smoothly.

⁴¹⁴ Hour: 22 is a little different than the other chapters of this book. It's a story of a man seeking advice on how to be a good husband:

¹(para.406) *Forgiveness can be extremely difficult at times, especially when a person carelessly or intentionally hurts you; and even more so when that person is your spouse. But if you're in the "marriage business" for the long haul, you have no choice but to forgive your mate (as quickly as possible).*

²(para.408) *Cruises are surprisingly affordable and they give you the opportunity to completely relax.*

³(para.410) *It seems that the world is so devoid of kindness that people are amazed even when they see ordinary, common courtesy. I was once offered 5 dollars by a man when he saw me hold the door open for an elderly couple. (I didn't accept it.) And I could have written a chapter in this book about the response I receive at restaurants when I pre-tip. When you show proactive kindness it makes that person feel like sunlight has burst through the clouds to shine especially for them!*

⁴(above para.412) *When making "deals" you can include more than one issue, but keep in mind that women are more willing to accept your offer if they are being fully supported. In fact, if your wife doesn't have to work outside the home, she may voluntarily stop doing things that annoy you when she realizes what she's doing.*

HOUR 22:
THE GOLDEN ROSE

Jason believed he had found the woman of his dreams. And even though he had only known her for 9 months, she had already earned his complete trust. Still, he felt uneasy because the topic of marriage has come up. His doubts about marriage didn't involve his girlfriend, Wendy. Instead, he felt unsure about his ability to be a good husband for such a loving woman.

He remembered what he had read in the Bible; that King Solomon prayed for discernment so that he could be a good leader. So he says a heartfelt prayer and when he opens his eyes, the phone rings. It's his Uncle Tim.

Jason: Hi, Uncle Tim.
Tim: How'd you know it was me?
Jason: Ever heard of caller ID?
Tim: Yes, I have. I also heard you were thinking about getting married.
Jason: Yes, things are headed in that direction, but---
Tim: But you're not sure if you'll be a good husband.
Jason: When did you become a mind-reader?
Tim: I don't know how to read minds, but I do know that all good men wonder if they'll be good husbands.
Jason: Do you have any Solomon-like wisdom?
Tim: I could repeat what I've told you all your life or I could give you a project to see if you've been listening to me.
Jason: I can use all the help I can get.
Tim: I'm going to bring you a "special" rose bush. I want you to plant the bush in your backyard. No one other than you can touch it. I'll return in a few months and if you've properly cared for it, I'll show you a golden rose.

Jason eagerly accepts the challenge and quickly gathers all the information he can find from the internet and the library about the proper care and feeding of roses. He buys the best soil he can find and plants the bush in his backyard to make sure it will receive the perfect amount of sunlight. Jason, in a stroke of originality, names the bush "Rosie". He waters and tends to his small garden constantly. Rosie is the most pampered plant in the world. Rosie grows quickly and Jason nurtures her every step of the way. He cleans every leaf, removes every pest and after a few weeks Rosie produces its first buds.

After another inspection, Jason calls it a day and goes to bed. A few hours after he falls asleep his girlfriend calls.

Wendy: Hey babe, I was watching the news. I think a storm is heading in your direction. I'm coming over to bring you something for Rosie.
Jason: Thanks, but you know that no one is allowed to help me with Rosie. Besides, a little rain won't hurt her.
Wendy: I know, but you don't understand.
Jason: Gotta get some sleep, babe. I'll call you in the morning.

Jason, a little miffed at Wendy for trying to break the rules, goes back to sleep. A few hours later Jason is again awakened, this time by a loud clacking sound on the roof. It's hail! Jason grabs an umbrella and rushes to Rosie. The hailstones are huge and have caused severe damage. He frantically searches for something to cover her with. As he races back to his garage he notices a tarp draped over his fence. He's not sure how it got there, but he doesn't have time to think about it. He grabs the tarp and a few poles and quickly covers what's left of Rosie. That's all he can do for now.

As the morning sun pierces through the clouds, it brings with it a ray of hope for Rosie. A few days later, after lots of mending, Rosie begins to sprout new limbs and soon she is almost as good as new. Weeks later Rosie rewards Jason for all his hard work with a grand display of red roses. Uncle Tim decides it's time to pay Jason a visit and when he arrives he too is dazzled by Rosie's brilliance.

Jason: Here she is, how'd I do?

Tim:	You did an excellent job. I can see that every leaf and petal has been cared for.
Jason:	I think I understand why you gave me this project.
Tim:	I thought you would get the point; that taking care of a garden is similar to maintaining a relationship. What did you learn?
Jason:	I learned a lot and many things you taught me were reinforced. As you've told me many times, a good relationship needs a good foundation, so I bought the best soil I could find.
Tim:	A solid foundation is a great start, how often did you tend to Rosie?
Jason:	I tended to her daily, or as you would say, I pampered her frequently. I made sure there were no weeds or pests on her or anywhere in the garden.
Tim:	I'm glad you added that last part. You knew to not only keep pests off the bush, but to keep the entire area around her safe.
Jason:	Patience. I knew that I could not force the plant to grow faster. I had to care for it the way it needed to be cared for.
Tim:	Exactly.
Jason:	Although it sounds strange, I developed feelings for Rosie. It seemed as though the more I gave, the more I cared for her, even though she didn't give anything to me. Is that what you mean when you said to give and expect nothing in return?
Tim:	Yes, but in all good relationships there's give and take. Just make sure you do your part since that's the only thing you control. But do you think Rosie gave nothing in return?
Jason:	Well I guess she did give me beautiful roses.
Tim:	Isn't that what you were expecting her to do? I hope you weren't expecting her to produce cherry tomatoes. That's where a lot of marriages run into trouble, when husbands expect their wives to do things they weren't designed to do. What rose bushes are best at is producing beautiful roses.
Jason:	Is that what you meant when you said that if all a woman did was be pleasing to your eyes, like a rose, that would be more than enough?
Tim:	Yes, but as you know women are more than just objects of beauty, they are loving, giving, kind, and wise. For example, I heard Wendy came to the rescue and helped save Rosie.

Jason: She did, but how did you know? Did Wendy call you?

Tim: Yes. When you told her you didn't want her help, she called me to see how she could help without breaking the rules.

Jason: Did you tell her what the rules were?

Tim: Yes.

Jason: Then why did she bring the tarp? Didn't you tell her she wasn't allowed to help me?

Tim: No I didn't.

Jason: Why not?

Tim: Because I didn't say no one could help you, I said no one besides you could **touch** the plant, which is what I repeated to her. Did she touch Rosie?

Jason: No, she didn't touch her.

Tim: So she acted wisely and lovingly by driving to your house after you hung up on her. But the fact that you wouldn't allow her to help you isn't the main problem, not listening to her is.

Jason: I don't understand.

Tim: You told me that you received a lot of information about caring for roses from the internet. If you thought no one was allowed to help you why did you seek advice from the internet?

Jason: I can't answer that.

Tim: And since you were willing to listen to advice from someone on the internet, why wouldn't you listen to your future wife? Doesn't she have a rose garden as well? Doesn't she have experience?

Jason: Yes, but Wendy's not an expert on roses.

Tim: It doesn't take an expert to know that hail can damage a plant. And had you listened to her, you could have taken precautions yourself. She would not have had to endanger herself by driving in a rainstorm to help you. And as for being an expert; I'm not an expert or a marriage counselor, yet you listen to me.

Jason: Yes, but you speak from---

Tim: From experience? You mean like Wendy? And which one of those internet experts drove to your house to bring you a tarp?

Jason: Now I'm really confused. What should I have done?

Tim: Listen. Just as you listened to the "voices" from the internet and deduced what they had in common. Simply add your future wife's voice to the equation.

Jason: I see I still have a lot to learn.

Tim: Don't worry. Just treat your future wife like you treated Rosie. After all, that was the point of the project. Remain humble and patient. Continue to search for wisdom. Make sure your marriage has a solid financial foundation so she always feels safe and loved and pampered. Appreciate her feminine beauty and don't expect your rose bush to produce tomatoes. And as you just learned, listen to her when she speaks.

Jason: I just realized that Wendy is the golden rose you wanted to show me.

Tim: Yes, she is.

Jason: How did you know she was going to bring over the tarp?

Tim: I didn't. Just like I don't know where lightening will strike when storm clouds roll in. The only thing I know is that when females are around love will rain down and I won't mind getting wet. I'd like to ask you something. If Rosie actually produced a golden rose, what do you think you would possess?

Jason: I would have the most unique, precious flower on earth. I would have to keep it safe, because it would be admired by everyone that saw it. I would give it everything needed so that it would remain healthy and soft. It would need me to be there every day to protect it from things that might hurt it.

Tim: Although they are often contaminated by man, both the female and nature are as close to perfection as they are allowed to be. So take care of your flower, she'll take care of the beauty in your life and she'll take care of you. Treat her like a delicate golden rose and you'll have a great marriage.

HOUR 23:
ADVICE FOR SINGLE MEN

> A wise person will listen and take in more instruction, and a man of understanding is the one who acquires skillful direction.
> Proverbs 1:5

⁴¹⁵ **They** say that those who cannot change their minds cannot change anything. If your relationships are not as successful as you would like, maybe you should look at things a different way. In this hour, I will discuss several topics to help you see relationships from a new perspective, starting with the idea that men are hunters. (Read carefully, because there's a test at the end.)

⁴¹⁶ Instead of thinking of men as hunters, I think a better description would be farmers; someone who cares for everything and everyone on his farm. Once a man has established his "farm" (in other words, he is stable financially) and wants to get married, he doesn't have to "hunt" for a woman. Financially stable men are as sought after as pure gold. And although hunting or chasing women is a favorite "sport" for a lot of men, if you want to get married (and stay married), you should:

Never chase a woman, instead, give her something special to follow[1]

⁴¹⁷ Good men and husbands are not hunters, they are providers and protectors. Some men may indeed like the idea of the hunt, but this method of "capturing" women is not the best way to start and maintain a relationship. Hunters stalk, kill and slaughter their prey. That doesn't sound like a loving courtship to me. I believe the idea that men are hunters partially originated from the mistaken belief that we were once dumb, savage, club-swing cavemen.

⁴¹⁸ If you go into marriage with the belief that men are hunters, do you suddenly stop hunting on your wedding day? If you believe it is natural for men to be aggressive and predatory, what does the future hold for your

wife? I believe that what a person does, is what they become. If you are a man who chases women, in most cases, that's probably what you'll continue to do.

419   The idea of the chase does not apply to women, because they are not animals; you don't "hunt" them. They are not a hunter's prey that is trapped and mounted on a wall as a sign of a man's masculinity. If you've read this entire book you should have learned that a man should treat a woman with love, understanding, and tenderness at all times!

420   When I say you shouldn't "chase" a woman, I mean you should never ask a woman for her phone number or any personal information and never, ever ask a woman you barely know for a date. If you are a fine, high-quality, financially stable man, women will naturally be attracted to you. Women are very intelligent and can spot a great catch a mile away. If you are a good man, it won't be long before she gives you all the information you need to contact her.

421   Women love men, you don't have to chase and badger them. The only thing women love more than men, are financially stable men. I'm not saying that women are gold-diggers. In fact, I don't believe true gold-diggers exist; women who love only money. I believe even a so-called gold-digger would love a man who loved and fully supported her, even if he wasn't rich. Women know that a financially stable man can provide security and protection for her and her future children. That's not being a gold-digger, that's being smart.

422   Chasing a woman means you have to convince her you are a good catch. Good men don't try to impress anyone, if they catch a woman's eye, she's already impressed. Women notice how men carry themselves and their behavior around others. Kindness, generosity, and helpfulness, endear, and impress more than anything you could ever say.

423   Trying to prove to a woman that you are a good man takes time and energy. And even if you convince her to spend time with you and eventually to marry you, you're forever left wondering if she truly loves you, because, after all, it wasn't her idea to begin with. She may not know her true feelings for you, because she may not have had the opportunity to examine the "real" you. Women want to fall in love on their own, they don't want to be convinced or tricked into loving you.

424   A woman who is being pursued may indeed feel flattered,[2] but she may also feel rushed and pressured to have "feelings" for you. She's being asked to show love to someone she doesn't know. Some women are good at faking interest to keep you around long enough so they can determine the real you. But pretending to like a man is dangerous, because most men can sniff out "fake interest".

425   Most men don't understand that this is a stall tactic. They falsely assume she is "playing games", when she is simply trying to slow down the relationship so she can get to know you. The budding relationship may be over before it begins, because trust wasn't established. But trust doesn't have a chance to develop if a woman is forced to go from stranger to girlfriend in a matter of days or hours! You may be a "great catch", but a woman needs time to figure that out for herself.

> **You accuse a woman of wavering affections, but don't blame her;
> she is just looking for a <u>consistent</u> man.[3]**
> Johann Wolfgang von Goethe

426   Unfortunately, many women feel pressured into relationships with men they don't really know. Heed this warning: Being involved with a woman who doesn't love you, may be as bad as being involved with a woman who's not sure if she loves you. The ups and downs will make you insecure and anxious. She simply isn't sure whether or not she loves you or even if she wants to love you. Not because she's fickle or playing games, she simply doesn't know you.

427   How can she be sure if she loves you when she wasn't given time to examine you on her terms? Instead, she was told she should love you and that she should believe what you tell her. Even if your relationship results in marriage, if the relationship progressed too quickly for her to really know you, you may have to spend lots of time and energy trying to prove to your

wife that you are the person you say you are. No one knows how long it will take before she reaches the same conclusion. In the meantime, trust may be eroding and as you've learned, there's no room for doubt and uncertainty in any kind of relationship and especially marriage.

428 A woman who is forced or rushed into a relationship knows she has to quickly convince herself that she loves you. Why? Because she knows she may have only one chance to win your heart. Until she feels true love for you, she has to stall for time by pretending to have feelings for you. She is forced to do things that don't feel natural to her, like measuring out love in small doses, just enough to keep you around until she's satisfied that you are truly deserving of all her love.[4]

429 Another reason you should never chase a woman is that it puts her in an awkward position. If she immediately accepts your proposition, she will be seen as "easy". On the other hand, if she rejects you, she may not get another opportunity to get to know you. Chasing women puts them at once on the defensive **and** the offensive. They have to run to appear hard to get, but they also have to give the impression that they are interested in getting to know you, but not "too" interested. (I got confused just writing that last sentence, imagine how confused a woman must be. She can't help but feel uncomfortable, stressed, and pressured.)

430 Chasing or pressuring a woman you hardly know, makes her unsure about you and her feelings for you. The only thing she knows about you is that you are aggressive. By being aggressive you may unintentionally send the message that your only motive is to take advantage of her; to get whatever you can, as quickly as you can. Being aggressive, as opposed to being patient and kind may make her feel as though you care only about yourself.

431 If you chase women, you will quickly become known as a womanizer, a man who has casual affairs with many women. You will have trouble simply starting a relationship and maintaining a relationship is almost impossible if you are seen as someone who is not loyal, honest, and trustworthy. (Even if you're financially stable.)

⁴³² Having causal relationships with lots of women will not only cause them harm when they are carelessly discarded, but you will also damage your own image of women. A woman who feels pressured into a relationship acts unsure because she **is** unsure. She is called fickle or a tease or crazy, because her heart tells her one thing, her mind tells her something else, and what goes into her ears (what you tell her) may all be entirely different. (Not to mention what her friends and other suitors tell her.)

⁴³³ What many men call crazy behavior, in most cases, may simply be confusion. She can't make up her mind and she feels pressured to quickly make what may be a life-changing decision. But know that once a woman is convinced you deserve all her love, she will give all she has to make the relationship work! All women may not consciously know how important trust is for a man, but they instinctively make changes to quickly fit into their mate's life. (I'll discuss the importance of trust later.)

⁴³⁴ Women don't take any kind of relationship lightly, especially intimate relationships. When you start a relationship with a woman you have to understand and accept that once she has agreed to be your girlfriend, marriage is the next step. But whatever title she may have, she knows innately that good relationships require harmony. They know that a strong bond must be made as quickly as possible, once she has agreed to blend her life with yours.

⁴³⁵ To sum up the preceding paragraphs, chasing women does not build trust for either of you. Chasing a woman sends many mixed messages, so is it a surprise that she acts "mixed-up"? You want her to quickly reveal her feelings for you, but not too quickly, because she would appear easy. You want her to act like a loyal wife though she hasn't even agreed to be your girlfriend. If want to pursue something, pursue a friendship. And instead of chasing women, work on being the kind of man a woman would want to follow. A kind, generous, financially stable 24:Hour Man!

How to approach women

⁴³⁶ Of course, you may be wondering how do you get to know a woman if you can't talk to her. I didn't say you shouldn't talk to a woman you're interested in; I said you shouldn't ask her for any personal information. (If,

and when she wants you to have it, she'll give it to you.) If you would like to get to know a woman, simply introduce yourself (and if possible, ask others about her). If she's new to the area, welcome her to the neighborhood or workplace. Ask about her family (to determine her marital status) and if she's single, let her know that she can come to you if she needs assistance, then go about your business and leave her alone!

437 In the meantime, if she is single and available, she will make it her business to find out about the gentleman who kindly introduced himself and offered to help her. That's all you ever have to do. (If she's single, she may be intrigued as to why you haven't asked for her phone number or asked any personal questions. Intrigued is not the same as confused, but call it what you will, the fact of the matter is, you'll be on her mind, in a positive way.)

438 But what about a woman you meet on the streets? First of all, you should never approach a woman on the streets. She could be married or a drug addict or nowadays, a man in a dress. However, if you just can't control yourself, again simply introduce yourself, tell her you would like to take her out as a friend if she's single and hand her your business card (that has your number and email address). Do not ask her for anything!

439 Think for a moment about the women who gave you their phone numbers when asked, do you trust any of them?[5] The answer is obviously no, because you don't know them. This is why I say you should get to know a woman first (by observing her and/or asking others about her) and allow her time to get to know you. In the meantime, what begins to slowly develop is trust, the foundation for all types of relationships.

440 Of course, many men think they have to move fast before another guy moves in and takes the woman he was interested in. Obviously, that may happen, but if a man catches the eye of the woman you were interested in, that may mean he has already laid the groundwork of friendship. But if he aggressively rushed in, that means they don't know each other and therefore, haven't developed trust. The odds are very high that they won't be together long. In the meantime, you're the one who's laying the groundwork of friendship. It's only a matter of time before she asks you for your phone number. You just have to be patient.

⁴⁴¹ Of course, aggressive men often convince women to spend time with them and many eventually marry. But, as you know from reading this book, if he is not financially stable, he has a decision to make. One, cut back on the time he spends with his wife so that he can become financially stable. Or two, continue doing what he did to win her heart.

⁴⁴² I'm sure you can see this man's dilemma. If he doesn't maintain his attentive ways, his wife, who has become accustomed to spending lots of time with her husband, will begin to think he's lost interest in her. This will result in her feeling less loved and therefore, insecure.

⁴⁴³ But if he continues to focus all his energy on pleasing his wife, he may not be able to build financial stability. Money problems will soon cause the husband to lose confidence and feel insecure. His wife will then reflect those same feelings. This is the situation many men find themselves dealing with when they are not financially stable before they start a relationship.

⁴⁴⁴ Though it may seem counterintuitive, the man who aggressively chases a woman is less likely to win her heart, compared to the man who spends most of his time building up himself, physically, spiritually, and financially. Women are attracted to men who are busy building a solid financial and spiritual foundation and men who are already stable.

Allow time for the relationship to grow

⁴⁴⁵ One reason women need time for a relationship to grow is because they are the ones who usually do most of the adapting in a relationship. They need time to see how they can fit into your life. (Obviously some women will want to speed up the process, but it's also important for **you** to know if she can adjust to your lifestyle and so it's important that you do not allow the relationship to progress too quickly.) Whether you are just a close friend or a significant other, she needs time to learn your likes and dislikes.

⁴⁴⁶ Allowing a relationship time to grow means building a foundation of trust by observing each other and aligning your lifestyles. Let's say, for example, you owned a bakery and you were looking to hire a baker. You have two candidates scheduled for an interview. They are told to bring the ingredients for a German Chocolate cake.

⁴⁴⁷ The first lady arrives, but instead of bringing the ingredients, she brings a finished cake. She states that this would speed up the interview process. Her cake is very well done. She even adds chopped pecans to the frosting, because she likes them, although they are not a normal ingredient. The second lady arrives with all the necessary items for the cake. You watch as she mixes the farm-fresh ingredients and melts the imported chocolate. She even grates the coconut herself. She also has nuts, but asks if you are allergic and if she should add them. She places the batter in the oven and soon the air is filled with chocolate anticipation. As the cake bakes, you have time to ask her questions about her experience. (She also gets to see how you run the bakery.)

⁴⁴⁸ Although the first lady's cake was good, you don't really know if she baked it. And because you didn't see her prepare the cake, you don't know how much she enjoys cooking. And the fact that she didn't ask if you were allergic to nuts may indicate that she is more concerned with pleasing herself than others.

⁴⁴⁹ As you can imagine, the second lady has a better chance of getting the job simply because you know more about her as a person, not just as a baker. You had time to observe her in action.

⁴⁵⁰ I can end the illustration here, because I'm sure you understand the point is not about cake, but allowing time to pass so that each of you has the opportunity to observe the other in action. You both need to know if the other is a generous and understanding person. Once a woman is sure you are genuinely a caring person (and financially stable) she'll figure out how to fit into your "bakery".[6]

Ready for marriage?

⁴⁵¹ Should a man who is financially stable aggressively pursue a woman who appeals to him? The answer is still, no. Just because you're ready for a relationship doesn't mean she is. Even if she has an initial attraction for you, she still needs time for what I call "pruning and weeding".[7]

⁴⁵² As soon as a woman becomes interested in a man she goes into "adapt" mode. She observes him and begins to transform herself into the kind of woman she believes he would be attracted to. For example, if she overhears him say one of his favorite colors is blue, she may add more blue to her wardrobe. If he likes long, straight hair, she'll let her hair grow if it isn't already long and straight. If he likes the natural look, she'll start "pruning" by wearing less makeup, for example.

⁴⁵³ She also knows she has some "weeding" to do. Men who regularly call her will suddenly find her unavailable. If the man she's interested in doesn't like the night-life, club owners will have one less patron and fitness centers will add one. These changes require time, which is why I have stressed that you allow time for relationships to grow. Once you are officially in a relationship, she naturally assumes you accept her as she is and believes she doesn't need to do any more "pruning and weeding". She can then focus more on learning your likes and dislikes, and figuring out how she fits into your life.

⁴⁵⁴ A similar analogy would be purchasing a car. Once you take it off the lot the dealer assumes you're satisfied. You can't return a few weeks later, and ask him to paint it a different color.

⁴⁵⁵ Unlike dealers in the car analogy, women, because they are very committed to their relationships, **are** willing to change, but changes take time. And since she believed you were satisfied with the changes she's already made, any other changes you ask for may be seen as an insult. This means if and when she makes those changes it will take a lot longer to accomplish. (Especially, if she's not being financially supported.)

⁴⁵⁶ Returning to the car analogy, once a car salesman has made a sale, any further interactions usually involve maintenance only. Likewise, once a relationship has begun women assume you are happy and so they concentrate on maintaining your happiness (not altering their appearance or personality). A few years after marriage is not a good time to mention you prefer blondes.

⁴⁵⁷   Had you allowed time for her to make changes before the relationship began, her desire to impress you would have inspired her to do almost anything. Losing ten pounds before the relationship started may have taken a few weeks, but now it may take a few years. And if you are not financially stable, and fully supporting her, they may never happen. A woman may feel dedicated to make changes for a man who loves and fully supports her, but what motivates a woman to change for a man who's not taking care of her?

⁴⁵⁸   Every type of relationship needs time to develop; this applies even more so in when it comes to marriage. The early stages of all relationships require lots of patience and lots of adjustments before two people can begin to bond. You can't learn everything you need to know about a person by going on a couple of outings. And you learn even less and are under more pressure if you refer to your outings as "dates".

Why you should **never** go on a date[8]

⁴⁵⁹   Never, ever go on a date and never use the "d" word. Call it anything you want, "power lunch", "food-tasting", "rodeo", whatever, but never refer to going out with a woman as a "date"![9] That word has probably destroyed more promising relationships than any other word in the dictionary. I say that because it immediately puts pressure on both of you to perform like a perfect gentleman and lady. You're expected to please a virtual stranger. It's as if you're being tested on a subject you know little or nothing about. Many great friendships could have developed if not for the pressure of the "d" word.

⁴⁶⁰   The stress of dating can be unbearable as each person tries to guess the likes and dislikes of the other, while appearing relaxed and charming. The date is always a single misspoken word away from abruptly ending. In many cases, relationships end before they start simply because of the color of a woman's dress or the type of shoe the man was wearing; things that don't matter when you're just friends.

⁴⁶¹   Dating has many unwritten rules that are different for each person. For some, dating means you date that person exclusively, for others it means you can go out with as many people as you want. Most people spend the entire dinner trying to figure out what the rules are, nervously trying not to touch areas that would offend their guest.

⁴⁶² For many people, dating means you are now an "unofficial" couple. As unreasonable as that may seem, it does make a little sense, because you are showing your companion how you would behave if you were "officially" a couple. And obviously, you wouldn't date other people if you were a couple. So, unless you want an instant relationship, I recommend avoiding the "d" word.

⁴⁶³ I'm not saying people shouldn't go out, just don't call it a d-a-t-e. Dating is an all-or-nothing proposition. That is to say, you go into it with the "goal" of becoming a couple. (This is especially true with women, so don't use that word that starts with "d" and rhymes with "eight".) There's very little chance that you will simply be good friends, because someone will feel rejected. If you want to get to know someone, go out as friends, or better yet, with friends. No pressure, everyone is relaxed and acting as normally as possible. It provides men an excellent opportunity to show the woman they're interested in what kind of person they are.

⁴⁶⁴ A woman can learn many things about a man in just one outing by simply observing how he treats others. She can observe if he uses profanity, if he over drinks, smokes, and if he is cheap. On the positive side, she can see firsthand if he opens the door for all the females in the party and if he pre-tips the waiter. This tells her that if he is this caring for his friends and strangers, he might be someone worth getting to know better.

⁴⁶⁵ You can make quite an impression on a woman simply with your actions. She just needs the opportunity to observe you interacting with others. She gets to know you on her terms. She may even overlook the type of shoe you're wearing.

Money, Marriage and Religion

⁴⁶⁶ How much money do I need to get married? Whenever I talk to men, that question is invariably asked. If you are living paycheck to paycheck, you probably can't afford to get married. There is no magic dollar amount to strive for to determine if you have enough to get married, but because men are logical thinkers, I will attempt to answer that question. But before I do, here's a trick question: What is the best day of the week?

⁴⁶⁷ The answer is pay day. The reason I asked that question is to once again stress the importance of being financially stable before you get married, because nothing gives a man that feeling of confidence like a pocket full of money. A confident man is a happy man. And a confident, happy, financially stable man is probably ready for marriage.

⁴⁶⁸ I say probably, because if pay day is indeed your favorite day of the week, it may mean you are not financially stable. Financially stable men don't get excited when they receive their paychecks, because it's just a drop in the bucket compared to the money they have in the bank.

⁴⁶⁹ If you want some numbers, here are some goals to reach for, before you contemplate marriage:[10]

1. A minimum of $25,000 in the bank (See "The Million Dollar Question" pg.94)
2. A good-paying job or your own business
3. A house (Not an apartment)
4. Life and health insurance
5. An automobile

⁴⁷⁰ When you have obtained the above and understand that if you get married, it is your duty to love and take care of your wife, you have a good foundation for marriage. If you don't believe it is your obligation to fully support your wife, it is the same as saying to her that you expect her to work until the day she drops dead! That's not the bright, promising future most women look forward to, but it's a sad fact for many of them.

⁴⁷¹ As important as religion is to a marriage, the reason I place so much emphasis on finances is because all husbands are obligated to provide for their families, whether he's religious or not. I recommend that a man have both a stable financial and spiritual foundation. But the religious man as well as the nonreligious man feels the same pressure when the bills begin to mount. Therefore, all husbands should be financially stable, preferably (say it out loud) **before marriage**!

Struggling DOES NOT make relationships stronger

⁴⁷² The myth that struggling together will make a relationship stronger was discussed in Hour: 6. As I have said over and over in this book, **men** need money to have a successful marriage. And to avoid a lot of the problems of adjusting to a new relationship, it is best if you are financially stable before you even think about getting married.

⁴⁷³ What makes the "struggling" myth so difficult to get rid of is the fact that women are so beautiful that many men lose focus and get their priorities mixed up. Instead of relentlessly chasing financial security, they chase the woman of their dreams. Many men also have the mistaken belief that struggling is good for marriage. Some women as well fall for the myth, because they are overcome by love's intoxicating sweetness. They then find themselves involved with men who aren't ready financially for a relationship.

⁴⁷⁴ Many women are indeed hopeless romantics and will gladly struggle with the man they love. One saving grace that helps her endure is the affection she receives from her husband. She can get a sense of security by clinging to him. And for a few moments, she can "feel" secure when her loving husband wraps his arms around her. It gives her the strength to face another day, to fight side-by-side with the man she loves.

⁴⁷⁵ Sadly, her knight in rusted armor is not long for the fight. Unfortunately, for married women, married men aren't good at struggling financially. They know that all marital responsibilities rest solely on their shoulders and that they don't magically disappear. Men don't usually have strong male role models to advise them. Most men don't have older, wiser men to consult with; someone that can assure them and encourage them to continue the fight. Instead, they battle alone, while the pressures of life and marriage build and build. Many men try to relieve the pressure by turning to alcohol or drugs. Of course, this won't fix the problem. If he can't solve the problems he faces when he's sober, he certainly won't fare much better if he's often intoxicated.

⁴⁷⁶ Are you happy when you struggle? Do you face tomorrow with a smile when you know the repo man is on the way and the electricity is scheduled to be shut off? If you believe, as I do, that women reflect what they receive

from their husbands, will your wife be happy if you're not? If you are not stable, how can your marriage be?

> **When you can't see the light at the end of the tunnel, create your own light!**
> T24HM!*2014

⁴⁷⁷ That's not just a witty phrase, it's a reminder that there is always hope. And that you should never stop searching for the light, because many people are depending on your bright, inextinguishable light for love and protection. Don't assume that no light exists because you can't see it. The good news is, there's always light within you and you can always find it if you never give up. Giving up is never an option, because as it relates to your family, the only light they see is YOU! If you aren't a guiding light, whose lead does your family follow?

⁴⁷⁸ I'm sure you now see that you can't be your family's guiding light without money (at least, not consistently). I hope you'll advise every man you meet not to get married until he is financially stable, because struggling does not make marriage stronger and it most certainly does not make marriage fun! Struggling financially makes adjusting to each other much more difficult. And adjusting to a woman who feels unsafe is almost impossible. This leads men to believe that women are hard to understand and difficult to live with. But the fact of the matter is:

Women are not as complicated as you think

⁴⁷⁹ Women aren't as complicated as you've heard. What makes them appear complicated is their reaction when they are not treated properly. For example, if you treat a mirror properly it will reflect accurately. If you don't care for it or hit it with a rock, you won't know what to expect when you look at it. Will it shatter into a thousand pieces or just crack? The only thing you'll know for sure is that it will reflect the treatment it has received.

⁴⁸⁰ On the contrary, women are easy to understand if you love them. If you whisper in her ear that she's God's most beautiful creation, will she not smile? It's only when they are mistreated that women become unpredictable or "complicated". A woman will respond to love and tenderness as surely as a rose will respond to sun and water.

⁴⁸¹ Here's one more important tip. Women live much more in the present than men. They pay more attention to what's happening right now, at this very instant. How you treat a woman from moment to moment is much more important than what you've done in the past or what you may do in the future. Just as the meals you eat day-to-day are much more important than the feast you may eat a month from now. Just as you wouldn't stop eating until that feast arrives, you need to make sure your loved ones receive love and affection, daily! To make sure you'll have a happy future take care of her needs today.

⁴⁸² Fully take care of your wife, pamper her and you won't have to deal with a "complicated" woman. If you are a loving, caring man it will be easy for her to love you, as easy as rowing downstream. Tell her often that you love her. Tell her that when you count your blessings, you count her twice! The most beautiful sight on earth is the face of a smiling female! Give her a reason to smile and she'll give you what you desire, but keep in mind that although she'll do whatever she can to be pleasing to your eyes:

Beauty ain't pretty!

⁴⁸³ The small room is cold and packed with women. The floor is covered with the remains of past victims; though there are no signs of struggle. Screams of suffering fill the air. One by one, women are taken to receive their "treatment", as many more bravely await their gruesome fate. Some have been waiting hours. The agony is expected, but no less excruciating.

⁴⁸⁴ The next victim is summoned. A peek behind the curtains reveal the instruments of torture. What will it be this time, toxic chemicals, blazing hot irons or razor-sharp electrified blades? A cloak is wrapped around the victim's neck, the time has come!

⁴⁸⁵ The hired gun approaches and washes the victim's head repeatedly so that the toxic chemicals can take their maximum effect. After the lethal chemicals are applied, it's time for the furnace. The victim's head is placed in a medieval gadget specially designed to keep the head intact, but put the brain into suspended animation. The victim has been successfully subdued, but this is only the beginning. After the subject's head is removed from the

incinerator and deemed ready, more sprays and chemicals are applied. There is seemingly no end to the torture!

⁴⁸⁶ This is not a scene from the latest horror movie. It's what many women go through on a regular basis; a trip to the beauty shop. Beauty is a full-time job, but the visit to the parlor is just one avenue to beauty. There's also makeup, jewelry, perfumes, and clothing. These things take time, energy, and money. The beauty process ain't easy, it's not pretty, and it's not cheap.

⁴⁸⁷ Many women must work this "job" and a 9 to 5, and take care of their families! That's three distinct jobs, not including looking after themselves by getting exercise and rest. Obviously, one of these jobs is not going to get the full attention it deserves.

⁴⁸⁸ Surely, you can now see that the workload for women is very heavy. A big burden will be lifted off her shoulders when you see to it that she doesn't have to work a full time job.

Two types of women: loved and unloved

⁴⁸⁹ As stated earlier, there are only two kinds of women: those that have been taken care of and those who haven't. All women may appear the same, but if you look closer, you'll see that their dresses are actually different shades of pink. Women who have been loved are usually more feminine, mainly, because they have been allowed to be feminine. They didn't grow up fighting and competing with men, instead they were protected and cared for. For the most part, women who been loved have very few problems adjusting to a loving man. She knows what a loving environment is and how a man is supposed to treat a woman.

⁴⁹⁰ On the other hand, a woman who was not raised in a loving environment does not easily adjust to any man, whether he's financially stable or a worthless bad boy. Just keep in mind that if you're considering a relationship with a woman who has not been consistently loved, she needs even more time to observe you to be sure you're genuine. She may find a relationship with the rotten boy easier, because that's what she used to; there are no rules, no requirements, no adjustments to make. Everyone is

looking out for themselves. But no matter who she gets involved with, the transition to being a wife will not be smooth. If you begin a relationship with a woman who has not been consistently loved and cared for, you absolutely have no choice but to be financially stable and extremely patient!

[491] Once you have achieved financial stability and are thinking about getting married, there is one secret quality to look for in a woman. I say secret, because many men don't seem to know that it is the most important trait to look for:

Do not marry a woman you do not completely trust![11]

[492] Marrying a woman you don't trust and therefore someone you don't love, will make it almost impossible for you to be a good 24:Hour Husband. Distrust is like kryptonite to husbands. It weakens your ability to love and give. If you are involved with a woman that you don't trust, it is possible that she may eventually earn your trust, but it may take lots of time. This is why I've stressed the importance of giving the relationship time to grow. Until she has shown herself to be trustworthy it is best just to remain friends.

[493] If you don't have complete trust for a woman you are considering marrying, it won't be long before your suspicions, real or imagined, destroy the relationship. In fact, if you do not feel she is honest and loyal, you will not be able to love her, no matter how beautiful and sweet she may be. Your heart and mind will be divided and soon, so will your relationship. The battle in your mind will lead to war with your mate. For men, nothing is more important than trust when it comes to marriage. If you don't believe you can trust the person who'll know your every secret, don't fool yourself into thinking you can fake your way through it. There aren't degrees to loyalty, either you're loyal or you're not.

[494] There are, of course, other qualities to look for in a mate. Every man has his own preferences, but if you start with trust, chances are good that your mind will allow you to love and care for the woman who has earned your confidence, even if she doesn't have all your preferences. Once you determine that a woman you're interested in is trustworthy, all her other qualities will be a bonus.

⁴⁹⁵ It is important that you understand that once a woman becomes more than a friend, you must be careful not to damage the trust she has in you by spending too much time with women you are not related to. It is also important to leave the past in the past. Don't refer to your past experiences (or hers) as secrets. There's nothing either you can do about your history. Once you have established trust, bringing up the past may destroy your future. Assure your wife or girlfriend that she doesn't have to worry about things that happened years ago. Instead, show her how bright the future will be. (See Hour: 21, pg.123 para.407-409)

The simple way to attract women

⁴⁹⁶ The road to a woman's heart is deceptively long; it appears closer than it really is, like a mountain in the distance. The journey is even more confusing, because the road to a woman's emotions is short. Men often convince themselves that a woman likes or even loves them because he can make her laugh and smile. But as I've said repeatedly, never chase a woman. You don't need to prove to a woman that you're a good man, she can determine that for herself, if she's given the opportunity. Women fall in love with who you are, not who you say you are. The road to a woman's heart is filled with men trying to take her love. They don't realize that stealing a woman's heart doesn't mean it belongs to you.

⁴⁹⁷ If you've paid attention you should know there's one thing you won't see on the road to a woman's heart. If you guessed a 24:Hour Man, you passed the test. Don't spend all your time and energy chasing a woman until she gives in because of exhaustion. When a woman determines (on her own) that you're worthy of her love, you'll know you've won her heart when, without asking, she gives it to you.

⁴⁹⁸ Many things you've learned about attracting women are wrong or at least, not the best way to go about it. Men spend lots of time and energy trying to convince women to like them when the job is already half done. Women are already attracted to men. But what makes a woman fall in love is the way a man conducts himself. Is he cheerful, gentlemanly, and does he show kindness to others? Does he dress neatly and appropriately? And of course, the easiest way of all to attract women is to do what you've read many times in this book, become financially stable.

⁴⁹⁹   Money itself is not what attracts women. You don't have to walk around in a suit made out of one hundred dollar bills! (Although you would attract a lot of attention if you did!) What attracts women is the confident way you carry yourself. Nothing is more attractive to a woman than a confident, yet caring man. Stability makes a man feel and act sure of himself. Women want to know more about him. One way to get to know him is to actually draw close to him; this is the very definition of attraction and you didn't have to lift a finger or say a word. Just be yourself and women will approach you, lured by the light of your confidence; the confidence that comes, in part, from financial stability.

⁵⁰⁰   Although I've said you should not chase women, I don't want you to think that a man should never be assertive. You just have to wait for the right moment. You have to watch carefully for those barely noticeable little hints that women give to let you know you have the green light.[12] You'll know when it's time to show her more of what you have to offer, when she melts into your arms and tells you she can't imagine life without you and that she wants to love you forever! Not exactly subtle, but that's the point; assume nothing! When you know a woman wants your love, then, and only then is when you make your move. When a woman makes it crystal clear she has strong feelings for you, when **all** doubt is removed, you can proceed with confidence, because as stated in Hour: 12, love is knowing. (I'm assuming that you are both completely free to start a relationship and you are financially stable.)

⁵⁰¹   Though society's values and ideas may have changed, our needs have not. We still want to feel loved and appreciated. But since our world is now so dangerous and unpredictable, women need lots of good men in their lives. They especially need their husbands to be heroes, to be 24:Hour Men; strong, confident, and reliable. They need the warmth of your light, because this world is getting darker and colder every day. You know the light is in you and it's as bright as the sun, you just have to let it out, consistently!:

[1] *(above para.417) Chasing women makes even less sense when you consider that women love men and aren't running from us. Most women will gladly allow themselves to be "caught" by the man of their dreams. One example of how prepared they are for marriage is the fact that most women already have a large collection of lingerie. They are patiently waiting for the time to wear it. If you show yourself to be a man of good character and you are financially stable, that's all the "bait" you need to catch a woman's eye.*

[2] *(para.424) <u>Note to women</u>: Though it may feel flattering to be pursued, there's a thin line between being chased and being stalked. Be careful when dealing with a man who enjoys chasing women, he may begin a new chase once he catches you!*

[3] *(above para.426) This quote was written in the late 1700's, which means that the idea that a man should be consistent is not new and that women know that a good man is a consistent man. Notice that handsomeness or position nor money is mentioned. What is meant by "consistent" could be many things, but when it comes to marriage, the only way you can provide anything consistently, is if you are financially stable. Note also that the quote says that a woman is "looking" for a man who's consistent. This once again shows that if you are a good man you don't have to look for (or chase) a woman, she'll find you!*

[4] *(para.428) Women love completely, that is to say, with their whole heart and soul. They know that giving love in pieces devalues it. Just as tearing off pieces of a one hundred dollar bill will soon make it worthless.*

[5] *(para.439) If you ask a woman you don't know for her number and she gives it to you, how do you know it's her actual phone number (or if she's given you her real name)? The answer is, you don't. Before the relationship has even started, doubt has crept in.*

On the other hand, if a woman approaches **you** and offers her phone number, you're not only sure it's a real number, but also you're sure she's interested in you. In fact, as much as we can "know" anything, you know she wants to get to know more about you, because women don't take relationships lightly. If a woman approaches you, you can be sure she's observed you and you've made a great impression on her. You can proceed with confidence, because you know where you stand.

⁶(para.450) *Though not scientific, I offer as "proof" that women want to observe men on their terms, the fact that rarely has a woman given me her phone number immediately after meeting me. But a few women have given me their numbers after weeks or even years of knowing me. Obviously, this means they have been observing me and only after determining that I was worthy did they want to draw closer to me. What about your own experiences, how often has a woman who knows nothing about you given you her number (without you asking for it)?*

Recall the arm wrestling story in Hour: 2, pg.24 para.91-92. The teenager quietly watched as I arm wrestled her friends. I didn't notice her, but obviously she noticed me. She took time to observe how I treated her friends and only after determining that I was approachable did she ask to arm wrestle me. I'm sure you can see that her goal was not to show me how strong she was (although she was very strong), but to draw close to me. She saw an opportunity to touch me, even though she risked injuring her arm. This is an example of how women observe men and find ways to get to know the ones they find interesting.

⁷(para.451) **Pruning** *means she'll stop doing things she discovers you don't like and start doing things you do like. She'll pay more attention to how she dresses and may even lose or gain weight. In other words, she'll make personal changes.* **Weeding** *means she'll make lifestyle changes; removing things from her environment that may cause the man she's interested in to distrust her, this usually means "weeding out" or removing all other male suitors.*

⁸(above para.459) *Another point on "dating". Many in society correctly believe that the point of dating is to get to know the other person. But as you've read throughout this book, I believe it's best to learn as much as you can about a person BEFORE you go out with them. When you do go out it's like spending time with a friend. And after spending time with your friend you both will have additional information that will help determine if the relationship will move to the next level. If it doesn't at least you have a good friend.*

9 (para.459) *Asking, "Do you want to go to the rodeo?", may be a good way to ask a woman if she wants to go out (as friends). When she asks what does that mean, tell her it's an expression meaning to go out to eat as friends. It can even lead to a discussion about The 24:Hour Man!. And if she's read the book, she'll know that you know how to treat a lady. (Make sure you remember to pay for the meal and pre-tip the waiter, because she'll be watching.)*

10 (para.469) *Many people will say that if every man had to have everything on this list nobody would get married. That may be true in some cases, but it may also inspire some men to focus on building a solid financial foundation. The point of the list is to help men understand the importance of being financially stable, especially as it relates to marriage. (This list applies mainly to US citizens. In some totalitarian countries men are limited as to how much money they can earn.)*

11 (above para.492) *I am assuming, of course, that you are financially stable before you consider getting married. If not, you won't be able to maintain trust for anyone (if you ever had it to begin with). When it comes to marriage, the connection between money and trust is extremely important. A man won't feel confident in his ability to consistently care for his family if he is not financially stable and invariably he will act erratically. His wife and family will assuredly reflect his actions. And when a man's wife begins to act erratically, he will begin to lose trust.*

Note that a woman may reflect your financial insecurity as well as your emotional insecurity. Many men are confused when they are very loving to their mates, but she is standoffish and cold. She is obviously reflecting financial insecurity. She can't consistently show an interest in sex and affection when she has to work and worry about bills, even if her husband is very affectionate.

Trust is earned over time and can't be rushed. When you have trust your relationship will be incredibly strong. Without it the relationship is weak and rocky, and never seems to gain any momentum. It's like trying to run as fast as you can while looking backward at the person behind you.

[12] *(para.500) Waiting for the "green light" is very important, because it signals not only that she wants to be in a relationship, but that she's available to be in a relationship. There may be several reasons why she is not giving you the signal, although she is obviously attracted to you. She may be in a relationship or just ending one. She may be pregnant or have small children that need her full attention. Or she may sense that you are not a 24:Hour Man and is hoping that in time you soon will be. Whatever the reason, wait for the green light! And while you wait, put all your energy into becoming financially stable, if you aren't already.*

HOUR 24:
THE SUN!

⁵⁰² **Absolutely** magnificent, awe-inspiring, and kingly. Often indescribable, with seemingly endless energy and power. Accomplishing the impossible, daily. Standing alone in silence, yet touching lives from a distance. A provider of the perfect light. Always at the ready to give to satisfaction, never asking for anything in return. A superstar in every sense of the word!

⁵⁰³ Maybe one day I'll write a tribute to the sun, but the words written above are for you. In fact, this entire book is a tribute to you. Like the sun, you emanate greatness simply with your presence. Like a ray of sunlight, there is power in every word you speak. You are a force with more potential than you can control. The only thing you need is God's guidance to use that sun-like power for the benefit of all those around you.

⁵⁰⁴ I am sure that becoming a 24:Hour Man is now one of your goals and I am you'll reach it if you believe, as I do that as long as you don't give up, you can accomplish virtually anything. If you read the Bible regularly, pray, occasionally go through this book, and imitate the sun's consistency, you will receive all the encouragement and instruction you need to reach your goals. Remember: When in doubt, do good, **HELP SOMEBODY**!

> **Men give advice; God gives guidance**.
> Leonard Ravenhill

⁵⁰⁵ I hope you will take my advice and strive to give as consistently as possible. An honest effort is all that's required of an imperfect soul. Man tries, God does! And because of God's perfect work, every man knows he was designed for something special. Great men are great because they give, consistently! If you are a husband, consistently love, support, and protect your family, because that's what great husbands do. If you give consistently, it is impossible to fail.

> **We don't fail because we intended to fail,
> we fail because we don't do what we intended to do.**
> Author unknown

⁵⁰⁶ Every man has an advantage over the sun. He can seek out those hidden in the darkness of poverty or loneliness. Clouds can block the sun, but you can brighten someone's day, every day! Visit hospitals, or donate to shelters. Carry an extra umbrella, canned food or clothing (a jacket, for example) in your car so that you are always ready to help.

> **A good man is like the sunrise, whenever you see him,
> you <u>know</u> he is going to brighten your day!**
> T24HM!*2014

⁵⁰⁷ Another advantage you have over the sun is that you can help create other "24:Hour People". Tell others about the importance of giving consistently and more importantly, demonstrate it! Pass along this book and encourage everyone you know to read it and to pass it along as well. Be a light that everyone wants to imitate. Strive every day to find new ways of giving. Give because those around you need you. The world needs more men of light to break through the clouds.

> **Be the change you want to see in the world.**
> Mahatma Gandhi

⁵⁰⁸ The sun is great simply because it consistently does what it was designed to do. If every man would **consistently** do what he was designed to do, (reflect God's love), it would be easy to see that Every Man is Great! There would be no darkness, because the earth would shine from the light of:

THE
24:Hour Man!*

*Sources: The Bible, Life and Logic

A good leader inspires people to have confidence in the leader, a <u>great</u> leader inspires people to have confidence in themselves.

Eleanor Roosevelt

A leader is one who knows the way, goes the way, and shows the way.

John C Maxwell

Before you are a leader, success is all about growing yourself. When you become a leader, success is all about growing others.

Jack Welch

Be ashamed to die until you have won some victory for humanity.

Horace Mann

40 Minutes:

RANDOM THOUGHTS

The Bible and belief in God

The Bible was printed in 1454 A.D. by Johannes Gutenberg who invented the "type mold" for the printing press. It was the first book ever printed. How many languages has the Bible been translated into? The Holy Bible has been translated into 2,018 languages, with countless more partial translations and audio translations for unwritten languages. (This is an enormous amount of translations. In comparison, Shakespeare, considered by many to be the master writer of the English language, has only been translated into 50 languages.)

When you look at the history of the Bible, you soon discover that even before you've read the first page, it is the most unique book ever written. Almost 5 billion copies have been printed! The Bible is the best-selling book of the year, every year! (25 million copies a year, US) It was written over a span of 1,600 years, by 40 writers, yet its message is harmonious throughout the entire book. Its very existence proves that there is a loving God, but it further proves his existence by providing prophesies and facts that weren't verifiable until centuries later!

It is understandable that many have given up their religious beliefs when you hear of the many violent acts done in the name of God and religion. However, giving up your belief in God should be the last thing you abandon. I say that because we all associate, to some degree, with an organization or group that we know is corrupt at some level: police departments, governments, and sports teams to name a few. But we still choose to accept them, flawed as they may be. Yet they hold no hope for everlasting happiness.

One more thought about the Bible, religion and a belief in God. Scientists are known for their disbelief in a god that watches over us, but of all groups of people, shouldn't they have the most confidence that God exists? I say this because they see for themselves the precise order of the universe and they know the astronomical odds that man could have come about through chance. They also know that mankind did not have the appropriate instruments to determine that the earth is spherical and "hangs upon nothing"; things taught in the Bible that no man could have known. Though they are the silent minority, many scientists do believe in God. But you don't have to be a scientist to see God's handiwork, just look around.

Faith Healers

If so-called faith healers could actually heal anyone, why don't they visit hospitals? They sidestep this question by saying that the person must have faith. Are they saying that no one with faith has ever gone to a hospital? Ridiculous as that is, why then don't they cure other faith healers, they certainly must have faith. (We could team up psychics and faith healers and have them drive around town. There would be no need for doctors. The psychic could tell the driver where a person is about to be injured and if they don't arrive in time, the faith healer could heal them.)

I have heard stories about religious leaders who have visited hospitals, followed by so-called miracles, but they all follow a similar theme. A period of time after the visit, usually days or even months, the person is "miraculously" cured. Excuse my disbelief, but this is not how miracle cures were performed in the Bible. There was not a time lapse. People who were cured had their health restored immediately, not hours or days or months later!

Are so-called faith healers con artists? Obviously, but I welcome any of them to cure my father, who has been dead for several years. Upon curing him, I will most certainly be among the believers.

Drug Testing

Why are athletes required to take drug tests, but doctors, pilots, and lawyers are not? They all have people's lives in their hands, though in different ways.

Hollywood, aka Cancerwood

In my opinion, there is nothing more evil on this earth than the modern, mainstream film industry. When it comes to normalizing and glamorizing sin, nothing comes close to being as depraved as Hollywood. I call it Cancerwood, because, like cancer, what it produces is deadly, spreads quickly, and there doesn't appear to be a cure.

There are many evil hotbeds on earth, but none compare to Cancerwood, because of its global reach. This "land of the lost" continues to churn out death-dealing poison at an ever-increasing rate. What it produces is like an invisible, cankerous gas, specially designed to engulf souls. I would advise all to flee this plaque spot and not look back, because Cancerwood makes Sodom and Gomorrah look like Disneyland. It not only promotes evil, it teaches it! This God-forsaken, white-washed grave excels in downplaying and normalizing sin. Anything goes in this evil junkyard. Every sin known to man is glamorized in Pagan City.

Cancerwood has now focused its attention on children, with movies like Harry Potter, which tries to convince them that there is a good side to witchcraft. The movie *Twilight* implies that vampires are real and deserve sympathy. More and more movies show children using drugs, drinking, smoking, and using foul language.

I could list hundreds of movies that illustrate the filth that Cancerwood spews out (like all NC-17 movies or, in my opinion, virtually anything by the Wayans brothers, George Clooney, Seth Rogen, Paul Rudd or Lee Daniels), but I'll focus on one movie that stands out as a "great" example of Cancerwood's expertise in normalizing sin. (I decided not to name this movie in case children read this book.)

This disgusting movie keeps in line with Cancerwood's insatiable desire to normalize sin and wastes no time in its quest to get the job done. In the very first scene, a woman involved in prostitution (I don't believe in calling women prostitutes), enters the motel room of a man and immediately pulls down her underwear. There is no conversation about the act that is about to occur, because this obviously happens regularly. (The man's father is also a "regular customer" of this lady.)

There are numerous messages that Cancerwood is sending in this one scene. First, that prostitution is normal and that there is nothing wrong with it; that it's easy and quick, just a regular job. It also continues Cancerwood's tradition of illicit sex between unmarried people. This occurs so often in today's movies that many are convinced it is acceptable for unmarried people to have intimate relations with no thought of the consequences. In Hollywood, a horror/fantasy movie would be a man having sex with his wife!

This filthy movie has many other levels of evil that it attempts to portray as normal, including racism and foul language. But this movie also showcases another disturbing trend that is becoming normal in Cancerwood. That being established actors accepting roles that require them to perform all manner of disgusting acts. This horrible movie is a perfect example of this. Virtually none of the established actors of "early" Hollywood would have accepted any role from this movie.

In this movie, the lead character, an established Hollywood actor, has sex with a woman involved in prostitution (this is implied, though not shown), he is a horrible role model for his son and also has sex with another woman he's not married to. This particular sex scene (almost 4 minutes long!) should have given this movie an "X" rating, but since Cancerwood is the Devil's playground, it didn't get one. (Note that Cancerwood has stopped assigning the "X" rating. They now use NC-17 in an effort to make trashy movies more acceptable.)

The female lead, again played by an established actress, is the willing sexual participant of the lead actor. This well-known actress is involved in one of the most disgusting movies I've ever seen and then wonders why her private life is such a public mess. What makes a person blessed with great beauty and a high level of success decide to do a movie like this may at first glance seem confusing, but when you take into account the fact that Cancerwood is devoid of morals, it all makes sense. People with no morals make movies with no morals.

When an actor tries to do the right thing he's scorned. I won't mention his name, but an actor was interviewed and stated that he was a married Christian man and that he would not do scenes that required him to kiss women. The interviewer immediately stated that this would keep him from getting acting jobs. In other words, like most people in Hollywood, it's more important to get an acting job than it is to show love and loyalty to a mate (not to mention God). Why am I not surprised?

Directors and producers share the blame in spewing poison over the entire world, but it is the actors who willingly allow themselves to be used like pawns. The vast majority of actors are ignorant, amoral, soulless accomplices, who beg for the opportunity to show what godless imbeciles they are. Many say they are just doing their jobs.

They often gather for any organization that wants to honor them. They revel in presenting themselves with awards to extol their great ability to spread filth. One by one these drug-addicted, hedonistic Jezebels, and tuxedo-clad buffoons stumble across the stage, faces smoothed and caulked with cocaine-infused pancake makeup to conceal their true Gollum-like appearances. They eagerly accept their precious idols and graciously thank the world for acknowledging their ability to further immorality. They do everything but invoke the name of Satan when they pledge to produce more vile "entertainment" in the future.

Hollywood is most certainly the devil's toilet and it's been backed up for years. Directors and producers are Satan's personal attendants. The actors are wading in the cesspool nearby, clamoring for the chance to star in his next production. With their foul-mouths filled with venom, they're all too willing to affirm that as Cancerwood's originality decreases, profanity and obscenity increases.

Hollywood proves that money is not the root of all evil. Instead, Hollywood proves that **evil** is the root of all evil. I say that because studies have shown that G-rated movies make far more money than R-rated movies. (11 times more in one study!) But Hollywood is so focused on producing garbage that it doesn't notice or more correctly, doesn't care.

Lewdness is not limited to Hollywood. Even rappers and their producers would rather spread filth than make money. If you ask kids if they would buy rap music if there were no swearing in the songs, all would say they would. But again, we have people in a position to do good who choose instead to further the normalizing of evil.

One final thought about Hollywood. Movie makers often build incredible temporary sets for their movies. They could contribute to society if they built or remodeled real homes, parks or buildings, and when the movie is finished gave away or sold them at a highly reduced price.

Computer Mice

Is it possible to use two or more mice at once on one computer? It seems it would be useful for collaboration and games. Remember "Pong"?

Alternative Lifestyles

Dr. Phil once told a male guest of his show (who was previously married with children) that he (the male guest) was "hardwired to be gay". ("Gay" is a euphemism I choose not to use, as I see nothing "gay" about being in opposition to God.) He followed that false statement by stating that the man had no control with whom he fell in love (and consequently, he is not responsible for the countless people he hurts). I have to assume that Dr. Phil believes that a person is created by God to prefer sex with someone of the same gender, as if this is some type of hybrid third gender. (Does a person who considers himself bisexual belong to a fourth gender?)

By using the term "hardwired", Dr. Phil has opened up a can with more worms than he could have ever fathomed. Who's to say that rapists, murderers, thieves, drug addicts, molesters, adulterers, etc., aren't "hardwired", and therefore, aren't responsible for their actions? Even worse, it implies that we should be understanding and accepting of any behavior, because they can't help themselves.

Dr. Phil (or Dr. Facilitate) has unwittingly (or wittingly) helped to perpetuate the lie that love and sex are the same and that you have no control over who you fall in love with; and therefore, no control over who you have sex with. It's debatable whether or not we have control over who we fall in love with (I believe we have complete control over who you fall in love with), but we most certainly have control over who we choose to have sex with!

Love and sex are not the same! Biblically speaking, sex was specifically intended for a man and woman who are married. No exceptions or loopholes or "backdoors". I don't think God **forgot** to add a provision for same-sex marriage or mistakenly said that sex between single people was unacceptable. By the way, same-sex marriage opens the door to child-molestation by allowing perpetrators to hide behind the cloak of marriage. I'll gladly support same-sex marriage when two men can have a baby.

The favorite rallying cry for many who live alternative lifestyles is that there is nothing wrong with loving someone. The insidiousness of this phrase is that it's true! It is the ultimate evil twisting of words. The fact of the matter is that you can love anyone you want, but you cannot have sex with anyone you want! This applies to everyone, no matter how you are "hardwired", because love and sex are not the same! Are you listening, Dr. Phil?

Talk about opening Pandora's box! Does this mean a man can have sex with a woman who's married to another man, because they love each other? This false loophole opens the door to limitless "opportunities"; no female (or male) regardless of age or relationship is off-limits. All that's necessary is for two people to scream that they love each other and then anything goes.

Finally, I do find it curious that Hollywood (the devil's lower intestine), does not often show men kissing in its movies and television programs, yet this is supposed to be an accepted way of life. Why is there such an uproar when this happens yet when two women kiss it's only slightly condemn or even joked about?

Prisons

Instead of getting credit for "good behavior", prisoners should have to work to earn early release. They should also be required to take courses so that when they are released they have a skill; thereby, making them employable and putting them in a position to pay restitution.

One more thought about prisons. A television program about a correctional facilities stated that cell phones are a major problem in prisons. (I wasn't aware that cell phones were allowed in prison.) My first thought was that I didn't know prison cells had electrical outlets; which are used to charge the phones. My second thought was, if cell phones are not allowed, why isn't the electricity shut off and why aren't cell phone jammers used?

Company Benefits

Why don't companies pay for life insurance for their employees? One example: a company offers to pay the premiums for a term life insurance policy 5 years in advance (Let's say that comes to about $2,500). In exchange, the employee makes the company partial beneficiary and returns the $2,500 should the employee pass away during the 5 years.

Obviously, a long term plan would work best and health insurance may also be included. For example, the company pays for a lifetime policy (and also health insurance, if possible) and is reimbursed all the money spent when the employee passes away.

Phony Psychics and Belief in Ghosts

Have you noticed that you rarely see two or more so-called "psychics" together? That's because they would each say something totally different and everyone could easily see that they were frauds. Here's a simple test: Line up 5 people (behind a wall so you could not determine their sex, age or race), all from a foreign country. Ask a group of so-called psychics to write down the names and ages of the five people lined up, as well as what they will have for dinner. Then check the results the following day.

So-called psychics seem to have the "amazing" ability to see things that happened hundreds or thousands of years in the past and the uncanny ability to "predict" the future years in advance, but can't seem to divine what happened five minutes ago or what will happen five minutes into the future. If they could actually talk to the dead, why hasn't one of them said who killed President Kennedy or any other well-known death? How about foretelling natural disasters like hurricanes and tornados?

While giving a "reading" psychics often asks clarifying questions, but if they need more information shouldn't they ask the spirit? Of course, no one can actually "predict" or "foretell" anything. So-called psychics very often rattle off a bunch of guesses, hoping that at least one is correct. When a guess is correctly "predicted" many are convinced that these con artists have "special powers". The best that any of us can do is forecast, like weathermen, using information we have around us. Gathering information and guessing at the likelihood that something will happen is what these scammers are actually doing.

Comedian Brian Regan has a very funny routine about so-called psychics and their "amazing" ability to twist words:

Phony psychic (giving a reading): I'm getting an "M", the letter "M"?
Man: His name was Bo Ziffer!
Phony psychic: **Mister** Bo Ziffer!?!
Phony psychic (continuing his so-called reading): He died of natural causes.
Man: He was shot in the face by a bazooka!
Phony psychic: So naturally he'd be dead.

To those who believe in ghosts:

- Is there a rule that ghosts must hide from the living? What can we do to them?
- How are you able to see a spirit if they're supposed to be invisible?
- What reason would a ghost need clothes? And why would the clothing be semi-transparent?
- Why would a ghost need a body or any visible form?

There is something that the thousands or millions of people who claim they've seen ghosts all have in common: none of them can prove it! Believing in ghost also brings up an interesting conundrum. If a person is killed and someone sees that person's ghost, should the killer be freed because the "deceased" isn't actually dead? Of course, this is a ridiculous argument, but believing in ghosts is equally ridiculous. People who are grieving will look for anything to ease the pain of loss and bloodsucking, so-called psychics are all too willing to offer "comfort" by saying anything they believe will get the most money out of people who are suffering.

Leash Laws

Most, if not all states, have leash laws, but wouldn't it make more sense to also require muzzles? And to maintain more control of our dogs, I recently discovered a new type of leash called an Anti-Pull Harness. It doesn't completely stop the dog from pulling, but definitely gives you a lot more control.

It's Better to Read More Non-Fiction Books

Although I believe we should read all types of books, I think we, as a culture, should concentrate more on non-fiction. Fiction or "cotton-candy books" as I call them, can lead to false beliefs and confusion. Many people, as a result of fiction reading, have come to believe in a myriad of ridiculous things such as ghosts, vampires and aliens. Have you noticed how massive some of these books are? Like cotton-candy they excite the eyes with their "fluffy" appearance, but offer little substance in comparison to their size. I believe the negatives far outweigh the positives when it comes to most fiction reading.

Fiction is for entertainment purposes only; you can't rely on any of it to be factual. Whereas non-fiction can entertain, inspire, and educate. I also highly recommend taking advantage of audio books (non-fiction, of course) as they allow you to "read" (and easily "reread") many more books.

Marriage Counseling

To put it bluntly, I do not believe marriage counseling does any good. Pre-marital counseling helps a little, but if financial problems exist, no amount of counseling will help. Many couples are told to give counseling a try when they fear their marriage is near the end. I believe this will only exacerbate the problems and at best delay the breakup. Marriage counseling is expensive and useless (in most cases). Unless the counseling is free and the counselor has a lead on a good job for the husband, it is a complete waste of time.

No offense to Dr. Phil, but most marriages would benefit more from a well-paying job than from a thousand of his snappy witticisms. A man who is financially stable feels good about himself and is in a position to take care of his family. In turn, a wife, who doesn't have to work outside the home, will take care of her husband.

A Radical Idea to Keep the Economy Moving Forward

Instead of small stimulus checks, the government could give the economy a huge boost if it gave each state 1 billion dollars a year. The money would be offered to its citizens as long term (10 to 15 years or longer), business loans (up to $10,000). The loans would be low interest (or interest-free if paid back within a specific time). That would mean at least 100,000 people per state, per year (a minimum of 50 million citizens over a ten year period) would have the opportunity to start a business (or simply pay bills). One of the advantages of this program is that the money that is paid back can be used to fund the program the following year; and in theory, cost taxpayers nothing!

Decriminalize Moving Violations

It seems strange that a person can be arrested for not paying a speeding ticket or any moving violation, when no one was harmed. Placing someone in jail for not coming to a complete stop seems to be a bit harsh. There are many other options that should be used before arresting someone for not paying tickets. If an offense doesn't "warrant" an arrest on the spot, why should a person be arrested for it later?

Ideas for the Airlines

- Offer bagless flights (or carry-on only).
- Instead of squeezing passengers who have missed their flights (or passengers who were bumped) onto another flight, airlines should have a few unpublished flights available.
- Use a mesh material so passengers can easily see if anything was left in the magazine holders on the back of the seats.

Famous Painters and Their Paintings

What makes a painting more valuable after the artist dies? Why is it that critics can't recognize the brilliant strokes of a great artist until the artist is dead? Vincent Van Gogh painted almost 900 paintings, but sold only one during his lifetime.

How to Decrease Car Theft

Automakers can make stolen cars undriveable, by designing power seats that slide forward as far as possible and tilting the back of the seat forward, when the car is turned off. The seat's back would block the steering wheel and the pedals, making the car undriveable. Any attempt to force the seat back will set off an alarm and/or disconnect the battery.

Fame

Many of us grow up wanting to be rich and famous, but from what I have seen of fame, it is not something to be desired. Mixed in with adoring fans are people who wish to do you harm and they can be indistinguishable. Fame imprisons you, it makes you wary of everyone you meet. If you are a family man my advice is to avoid fame, as it places everyone in unnecessary danger.

Rating Media

Why aren't books, magazines, live performances, and radio programs rated like movies? In case you didn't notice the rating on the cover of this book, The 24:Hour Man! is rated G.

Oprah Winfrey

Although I admire Miss Winfrey for all the good she tries to do, as in the case of Dr. Phil, she may be causing just as much harm as good. For example, she proclaims loudly how much she enjoys being single. This in itself is not bad, but the fact of the matter is she is single and unattached only in the sense that a Wi-Fi connection is not attached by wires. You can do as much with Wi-Fi as you can with a wired connection. Likewise, Miss Winfrey is in a relationship and is doing almost everything a married woman does with her husband.

My problem with Miss Winfrey is not that she lives with a man she's not married to, that's her business. My major problem is that she tells the world how much she enjoys being single, while she enjoys all the benefits of marriage. This sends a misleading message to women who want to get married. How confused they must be. A woman they admire tries her best to convince them how great the single life is, although she's not really single! Single women know how hard and lonely it can be to be "truly" single.

I also have a minor problem with Miss Winfrey's book club, or more specifically her choice of books. As you've previously read, I think more attention should be paid to non-fiction books. The vast majority of her suggestions are novels. This means that millions of hours are wasted reading fantasies. Imagine if most of those hours were spent reading non-fiction. To be fair, Miss Winfrey has recommended a few non-fiction books. One in particular is a book (**I do not recommend**) by Eckhart Tolle called *A New Earth*. What makes this book an odd selection for her book club, other than the fact that it is a work of non-fiction, is that the author repeatedly refers to Jesus. I say this is odd, because Miss Winfrey is not a believer in Jesus, yet raves about a book that uses the teachings of Jesus to prove its points! That's like a vegetarian making soup with beef stock.

Aliens and Space Travel

Aliens can be added to the list of outlandish beliefs many people have been convinced of, because of works of fiction and sci-fi movies. There is absolutely no proof of aliens, but some people are absolutely certain of their existence. They base their belief on the incredible number of objects in space. However, simply knowing that objects exist in space doesn't prove life exists on them. Conversely, if space appeared to be completely empty, besides the sun and earth, that wouldn't be proof that life doesn't exist elsewhere; as there could be life outside our view.

Just a little thought will reveal that even if life existed on other planets, the distance alone makes it impossible to get there. Let's look at some numbers. Fiction books and TV shows like *Star Trek* give many people the foolish idea that an object can travel at the speed of light or faster! Let's assume we could travel at the speed of light, approximately 670,000,000 miles per hour. (In case you're wondering, the speed record for a manned vehicle is only about 25,000 mph. This means that even if you multiplied the speed record times 20,000, you still wouldn't be close to the speed of light.) To reach the closest galaxy to ours, traveling at the speed of light, would take about 25,000 years, so pack a lunch. I don't think many people will volunteer to take a 50,000 year round-trip into space. But maybe technology can achieve speeds 1000 times the speed of light and cut the travel time down to only 50 years (round-trip).

The idea of bounding around through space and finding a planet with life is even more ridiculous, because there are billions upon billions of objects in space. As you can imagine, the odds of finding a planet with life are outrageous. Additionally, if there is no life on the planet you visited, you'd have to travel another few thousand light-years to one of the other gazillion planets. Here's a question: if we are unable to "signal" other planets, what makes some people believe we can travel there? We can barely make it to the moon and back, and it's in our own backyard!

As you can see, even if we could travel at those ridiculous speeds, the time it takes to travel to other galaxies would make it impossible to reach them. And that does not take into account food, air, and fuel. Like many things, if we would do a little research we would realize that many things we believe in simply aren't true or feasible.

Concerning the existence of aliens, some people believe aliens came to earth and built the pyramids. This would mean that they traveled billions of miles and hundreds or thousands of years to get to earth and then built a pile of blocks. Does that sound logical?

Time Travel

Works of fiction (and Hollywood) have caused many people to believe many crazy things, time travel is one of them. The idea of going back in time is absolutely ridiculous, but fiction writers have sold many on its possibility, so I'll discuss it.

Let's start with the insane idea that a machine could be made or a portal exists and someone could be sent 200 years into the past. (How it's determined how far you went back in time and where you went, are also ludicrous thoughts to entertain. Also, how would you get back? I guess you could take a portable time machine with you. Of course, you couldn't go back to a time that didn't have electricity to power the time machine; unless it was powered by batteries. This argument is getting more and more ridiculous!) Many have said that you wouldn't be able to change the past because it's "locked". But no matter what you did or didn't do, just by being seen or heard it would change history, at least the history of the person or persons that saw you. Even the ground you walked on or the air you breathed would change history.

Traveling to the future is even more ridiculous, not to mention impossible. You can't go to the future, simply because there's nothing to go to! You can't go to a place that doesn't exist. (I suppose this applies to going back in time as well. You can't go back to a time that's gone.) The future hasn't happened, so how could you go to it? Even if you could go to the future there wouldn't be anything alive because it hasn't been born or created yet. The only thing traveling to the future would be you.

Sports 2.0

To make sports, like soccer, volleyball, and hockey even more exciting, add a second ball or puck. Make one ball black and give two points if it scores. Make the other ball or puck red, it earns one point. Raise the net in volleyball (to eliminate spiking) and give teams unlimited attempts to get the balls over the net. In soccer, add a second goalie or give another player or players the right to assist the goalie.

Thumbprints

Shouldn't thumbprints be applied to any document that requires a signature? This would help settle many disputes.

Ideas for Schools

- Instead of having separate schools for girls and boys, wouldn't it be simpler and cheaper to have separate classrooms?
- There should be a one large collection of audio books that all schools and colleges can access.
- Vocabulary should be a separate and required course for all students, from the 1st grade through high school.
- Classes for all ages should not begin before 9:00 a.m. If possible, school doors should open at 6 a.m. and close at 9 p.m.

While watching game shows I noticed that some days I would be able to answer several questions and other days I could answer very few. This got me thinking about how tests are administered in schools and what may be a better way to give tests.

If tests had 10-50% more questions, this would allow more leeway for missed answers. For example, instead of 10 questions on a test, the student would be given 15. Grading would remain basically the same. Five correct answers would equal 50, six correct answers would equal 60, etc.; and 10 or more correct would be scored 100. This would encourage students to keep trying even though they may not know the answer to a few questions. Additionally instead of asking, "Who knows" the answer to a question, students should be asked, "Who doesn't know" so that they can receive more instruction.

A tip for students (from Michel Thomas): When trying to determine whether a word is a verb, noun or adjective, use this tip. If you use "to", as in "to run" or "to play", it's probably a verb. If you use "the", as in "the phone", it's probably a noun. If you use "is" or "am", for example, "my dog is tired" or "I am bored", it's probably an adjective.

Gangs

Why is it so difficult to get rid of gangs? They gather in groups and all wear the same colors! If they were followed for a couple of days or weeks, eventually they will commit a crime and over time all gang members would be in jail. Depending on the crime committed, the length of their sentence would be based on how long it takes for them to learn a skill.

Recommended Reading

Ultimate Secret to Getting Absolutely Everything You Want
by Mike Hernacki

Page-a-Minute Memory Book
by Harry Lorayne

For health tips:
www.Mercola.com

Idea for Auto Makers

Place a sensor on the front of the car that monitors the distance of the car ahead. Put a display on the dashboard that alerts the driver when he is within 2 seconds of the preceding car. This would help drivers follow the 2-second rule.

How to Reduce Pharmacy Mistakes

If the label on bottles of medication had a large color picture of the pills that are supposed to be in the bottle, mistakes could more easily be caught by the pharmacy staff and the patient.

How to Stop Money Counterfeiters

Round off the corners of the bills, gild the edges blue on the top and red on the bottom. Use more colors, such as gold or silver. Though not necessarily for security reasons, a bar code could be added.

DNA and Memories

I was asked an interesting question about memories: Is it possible that memories of our ancestors are stored in our DNA? This would probably explain why people claim to have lived past lives.

Natural Sweeteners

Why don't soda makers use natural sweeteners? Even if they cost a little more I'd at least like to have the option. I'd like to try 7UP with stevia or Pepsi with xylitol or Sunkist with honey.

Dumbing Down

A movie released in 2006 has as its premise: "stupid people have out-bred intelligent people." However, it seems the truth is that intelligent people are getting dumber or at least acting dumber and this is the bigger problem. It is the "dumbing down" of intelligent people that we have to worry about. You can't "dumb down" someone who is already uneducated. More and more I hear of seemingly intelligent adults becoming engrossed in mindless video games and many spend hours reading and talking about comic books.

It seems that "dumbing down" could potentially take hold of our culture if we continue the trend of elevating people who specialize in only one area, while ignoring all other areas of expertise. We may then end up with a society of people who are not well-rounded and are therefore, more easily manipulated by people who specialize in another area. Needless to say, people who concentrate on one field of study and then spend countless hours on mindless pursuits like video games and comic books don't have time for the more important things in life, like taking care of others or even their own health. And they certainly don't have time for religion. What we would then end up with would be selfish, over-weight, and amoral people. It is this group which should cause us the most concern.

This relaxing of standards and "dumbing down" affects many areas of our culture. For example, we have people in high positions who don't dress properly or who dress too causally in public. This influences others to relax their standards.

The Handshake

All boys should be taught how to properly shake hands. I have "popped" the hands of several men because they didn't know how to shake hands. Many women have given me better handshakes than some men.

Questions About The Big Bang Theory and the Theory of Evolution

I heard a man question that if the universe began with a big bang, why are all planets round? I have other questions:

- Why is all matter traveling at virtually the same speed, billions and billions of years after the so-called big bang?
- Why has the Earth been revolving at virtually the same speed for billions of years?
- What is "powering" our movement so precisely and continuously?
- Is it possible that there could have been several "Big Bangs"?

Questions for evolutionists:

- Did animal and plant life originate from the same cell? If so, do plants evolve? Also, which came first, animal or plant life?
- Has the "chicken or the egg" question been answered?
- If it's a fact, why is it still called a "theory"?
- If we came from cells, when did we become self-aware? In other words, when did cells realize they were cells? Or later in the so-called evolutionary path, when, if ever, did apes realize they were apes?
- If evolutionists doubt that there is a God because they believe there is no proof of his existence, why then do they believe in the Theory of Evolution, as it most certainly has not been proven?

I believe many evolutionists confuse "adapting" with evolving. Be that as it may, if evolution had truly been proven, as many evolutionists insist, where is the "headline"? Every newspaper in the world would have had that story on its front page if it had been proven. The greatest story of all time, proof that mankind originated from a single cell, would not be ignored. That would be like the moon being torn in half by a comet and no one reporting it!

The "Cure"?

I have noticed that when I'm busy doing something I enjoy, I don't think about eating or sleeping or worrying about problems. In other words, I'm not focused on myself. I experience the same feeling when I help others. This leads me to believe that the "cure" to feelings of loneliness and depression is to keep busy helping others and doing things we enjoy.

A Message to Atheists

If you are a person who does not believe there is a God, are you shocked when you are a victim of a crime? Are you surprised when you see people treat others inhumanely? Though it may not ease your mind, I have good news: since you believe there is no ultimate authority on good and evil, that means we are all gods. We decide individually what is right and what is wrong. Actually, "demi-god" or "semi-god" would be a better description, as we are not all-knowing and can't seem to solve those pesky problems of aging and dying. (Even if we were immortal, the question of where we came from would still need to be answered.)

In regard to my original question, how do you react when someone attacks you? Are you accepting of his or her actions? Shouldn't you be understanding of anything anyone does to you? After all, as gods, we can do whatever we want to do. Of course, you can complain, because you're a god as well. However, I have the right to smack you in the mouth for complaining, because I hate complainers. See how that works? The only rule is, there are no rules. Just do unto others before they do unto you. Isn't that what is meant by survival of the fittest? A godless world means we have a society made up of individuals who each have their own idea of what is good and bad, it does not and cannot have a unified voice. A society like that is profoundly incapable of finding permanent global harmony.

So the next time someone robs or shoots you, don't complain, just give 'em a high five and say, "You got me", because if there is no god, there is no ultimate judge of right and wrong. Just enjoy the world you've helped to create and return to the dust in a few years. In a godless world, don't expect justice, because the person who "wrongs" you is also the judge and jury, so I doubt he'll rule in your favor. And depending on his mood, he may also be your executioner. So live for now, because you'll be dead a long time.

One more thought for people who believe religion is the cause of many of the problems we face. Russia is probably the most godless country in the world and yet they have just a much crime, poverty, and governmental corruption as the US. This means that getting rid of religion will solve nothing and will, in fact, make things much worse. As corrupt as many religions may be, I doubt that the gang that terrorizes your neighborhood is a group of Bible students. They're more likely to be atheists and agnostics.

Charities

As much as I believe in helping others, I am very reluctant to give money to charities. I believe we need to change the way some charities are structured.

Many people work tirelessly and give generously to charities that have produced little or no results. To make matters worse, charities are not required to show how the money is being spent.

Instead of giving money directly to the charity, all donations should go to a bank or a savings institution. When the charity shows what items are needed to be purchased, they are given money that has accrued from the monthly interest; the principal is never touched. (Obviously this won't work for all charities.) If the charity is no longer needed, the money is then given to the fund of other charities. This would eliminate or at least cut down a lot of waste and corruption.

Hello Day

There are almost 7 billion people on earth, yet many people are lonely. We have multiple ways to connect and communicate with each other, but many still feel disconnected. Though we try to meet new people through email, text, and cell phones, they are not the best way to get to know someone. Those forms of interacting are only parts of the communication/relationship process; just as vitamin and mineral pills are just small parts of fruits and vegetables. Obviously we need the whole fruit, so to speak, to feel truly connected to someone. We need to touch and see them. What would happen if one day a month we all said "Hello" (or "Hi" or "How are you?") to at least one person we didn't know? Let's make the first day of every month, "Hello Day".

FAQ

I intended to answer a few questions concerning the merits of The 24:Hour Man!, but I think I covered every area I possibly could.

The one question I will answer is, "Will my relationships improve?" Obviously, I believe the answer is, yes, but only if you follow these instructions:

1. Apologize for not living up to your wife's dreams.
2. Get your finances in order so that your wife doesn't have to work outside the home.
3. Pamper your wife, frequently! (See Hours 18 and 19, page 105)

Many men have challenged me, stating that they don't believe this approach will work. They, of course, haven't tried it. The only way to know for sure is to do it. So go ahead and prove me wrong, take all the time you need pampering your wife, I'm sure she won't mind.

HOUR 25:
FOR WOMEN ONLY!

I had not intended to ever write another book after this one, as I do not enjoy the writing process. I originally intended to write a few pages in Hour: 25, but since most women don't receive the praise they deserve, a few pages would not be adequate; an entire book of praise would be more appropriate. I believe every woman deserves to be loved and made to feel special, but many women will probably never meet a 24:Hour Man in their lifetime. And since I can't personally pamper every woman on earth, I decided the best way reach as many women as possible is to write a book, a book **For Women Only**! It will be my "personalized" gift to you.

It will be called **The 24:Hour Woman!**. Unlike this book, which is my attempt to inspire men to behave like men consistently (24 hours a day) and to give of themselves consistently, it will be a book filled with good news and encouragement. Women don't need to be told to give, that comes naturally. Instead, your book of praise will contain poetry extolling the beauty of the female, God's most beautiful creation. It will contain advice on how to identify and attract only 24:Hour Men and how to deal with the men in your life who are not 24:Hour men. It will be a book of appreciation, comfort, and most of all, adoration!

I will give my opinion of Steve Harvey's heartfelt book, *Act like a lady, think like a man*. One major difference between his book and my soon to be written book is that I will strongly encourage women to avoid men who are not 24:Hour Men; whereas his book gives advice on how to deal with them and how to "train" them. (Boys need training, not 24:Hour Men.) He states that women don't understand men and while I agree that women don't totally understand men, they know enough. The biggest mistake women make is getting involved with men who are not emotionally ready and more importantly, as you've read in this book, aren't financially ready to be in a relationship. I will advise repeatedly **not to get involved with a man who is not financially and emotionally stable** and to be careful even befriending men who are not stable.

The female was designed to be the epitome of beauty and a beautiful flower is what you are! Nothing can stop the Amazing Female from blooming! But you can make it easier to bloom by associating only with people who are positive. And when choosing a partner, don't attach yourself to anyone who doesn't want to treat you like a queen and who doesn't appreciate your feminine qualities. That will be one of the messages in *The 24:Hour Woman!*.

Your gift will be available soon and as you shouldn't have to pay for your own gift, I will accept no profit from ***The 24:Hour Woman!***. All funds above production costs will be donated to charity. So until your gift is ready:

Make sure **EVERY** male you know reads:

The 24:Hour Man!*

Coming soon!:

The 24:Hour Woman!*
For Women Only!

It is my personalized gift to you!

*Sources: The Bible, Life, and Logic

www.ingramcontent.com/pod-product-compliance
Lightning Source LLC
Chambersburg PA
CBHW080339170426
43194CB00014B/2626